The Rebutted Presumption

Why Americans are exempt from and U. S. persons are liable for the federal income tax

James Bowers Johnson

i

For the Unenlightened

Disclaimer

Nothing in this publication should be considered legal advice. If you want legal advice, contact one who practices within the *legal* profession. <u>The Rebutted Presumption</u> is an effort to pursue the truth within and without the legal realm, which is fraught with the obscure, undefined, and misunderstood. If you seek truth, discern the content provided herein.

Note: All bold text in any citation is for emphasis.

Appreciation is given to David Pruss, creator of the illustrations.

Table of Contents

Preface

My mother encouraged me to write a book about federal tax law and jurisdiction that could be understood by those with a sixth-grade education. This feat requires correct definitions of legal terms and their limits of application. For, if sixth-grade students are to comprehend new and simple concepts, they must have a foundation upon which to build. In order to comprehend complex statutes, regulations, and law, they must know fundamentals. Moreover, they must unlearn or disbelieve what they already think is true. Given human nature, this is invariably impossible.

It is not easy to unlearn what we *know* is correct, much less learn something completely contrary. For most people, the idea that Americans are not liable for the federal income tax is untenable. The reason is simple. As a people and as individuals, we fear the IRS and government. We fear until we submit on a wholesale basis. Why do we dignify a fear which is without merit? We do not know truth. The truth is that the issue is not about taxes; it is a matter of jurisdiction. If the IRS does not have jurisdiction, there can be no tax and, thus, no reason to fear.

Our challenge becomes rather axiomatic. To prevail against unconstitutional actions of the Federal Government and its austere agencies, we must overcome ignorance, disbelief, and lack of courage. This is no small matter. As we proceed, let's embrace the definitive understanding that the government controls only what it creates or what it is able to influence within its scope of powers cited under Article 1, Section 8 of the Constitution. Beyond these powers, the government may not venture, unless done so brazenly and without accountability.

If Americans understand jurisdiction and that they are not liable for the federal income tax, why are they denied the possibility of a reasonable defense in court in criminal tax trials?

Keep this query in the forefront as we contend with government deception and what we are about to learn.

If a picture is worth a thousand words, the following graph tells a tragedy. From 1776 until the 1920s, expenditures on behalf of the United States Government were negligible. The escalation of debt from the 1940s into the 1970s became prohibitive, while hyper-spending into the present became farcical.

This graph reflects *what* happened; but it does not explain *why*. Extreme spending by the Federal Government is one thing; understanding the *source* of the funds is quite another. What is the impetus for these egregious and unconscionable outlays? The government was fiscally accountable before the 1930s. Yet, today, the government is reckless. President Obama and his government added over $9 trillion to the federal debt, a sum greater than $75,000 for each working American.[1] If the amount of a country's debt reflects its weakness, America's strength is no more.

If we examined graphs for any number of issues, we would glean equally troubling conclusions. America is an empire in decline. To illustrate, America is the most obese country in the world[2]. Americans are the most incarcerated globally.[3] Excellence in education is no longer near the top of industrialized nations.[4] Finally, with a ranking of 23 for all countries, America's standing as a *free* people is no longer a distinction.[5]

---

[1] http://www.thenewamerican.com/economy/commentary/item/25188-national-debt-under-obama-grew-by-9-trillion-86-percent
[2] http://health.usnews.com/health-news/health-wellness/articles/2014/05/28/america-tops-list-of-10-most-obese-countries
[3] https://www.washingtonpost.com/news/fact-checker/wp/2015/07/07/yes-u-s-locks-people-up-at-a-higher-rate-than-any-other-country/?utm_term=.8bbd927668d7
[4] https://rankingamerica.wordpress.com/category/education/
[5] https://www.cato.org/human-freedom-index

This book invites the unsuspecting reader to question what is hidden within the nuanced, distorted, and undefined. It seeks to illustrate those concepts which have an obvious black and white contrast. If we are able to admit our ignorance of a given topic and willing to concede that our beliefs are neither true nor objective, we may learn why America's core principles have been compromised. If a free people are whipped about by winds of senseless change, if a free people become unmoored from fundamental tenets, if a free people no longer exercise power inherent with their standing as the source of sovereign authority, the adverse extremes reflected on any and all graphs will reveal their eventual tragic end.

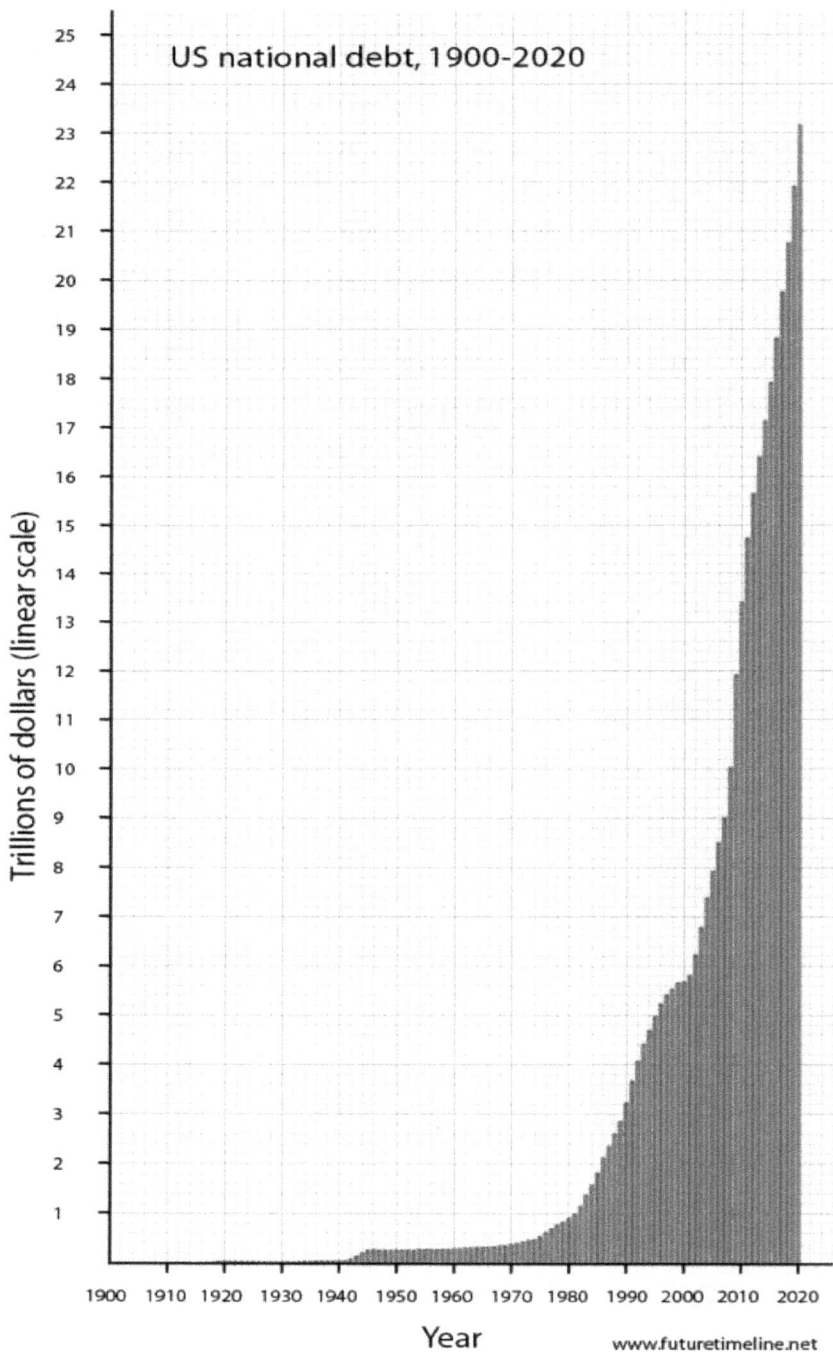

US national debt, 1900-2020

www.futuretimeline.net

x

Pre-Test

Identify as True or False:

a)   The United States is the several States, the 50 states of the Union.

b)   Americans may be within the several States and never step into the United States.

c)   Americans may not step into the United States while being within the jurisdiction of the United States.

d)   Americans may step into the United States without being in or under the jurisdiction of the United States.

e)   The United States is a legal fiction created and distinguished by language.

The Concept of Jurisdiction

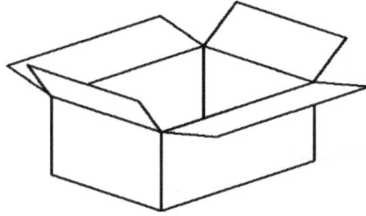

This is a box.

Within

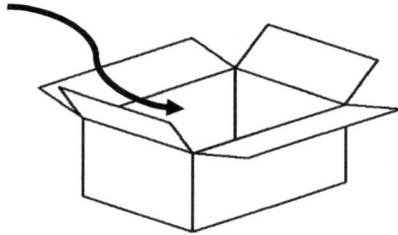

Anything inside the box is within.

Without

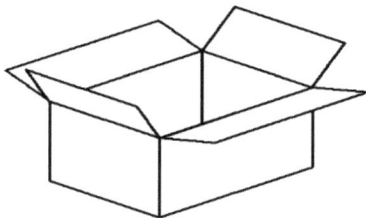

Anything outside the box is without.

Within

Within means inside, a part of, or included.

Without

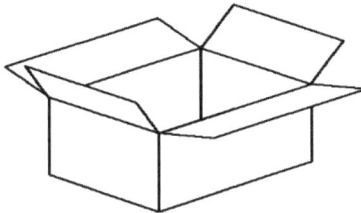

Without means outside, separate from, or excluded.

Without

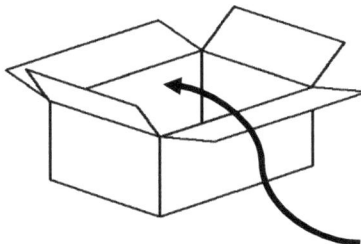

Within

Everyone and everything not within, a part of, or included is without.

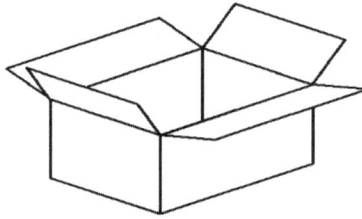

If you receive a box in the mail, it includes whatever is within.

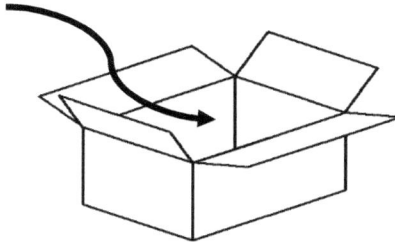

Vegetables

If vegetables are within the box, including carrots, onions, and turnips, all else is without.

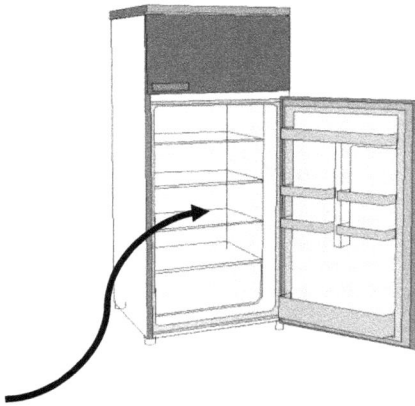

Pears

If a refrigerator includes only pears, nothing else is within.

Within

Suppose you make a salad with the vegetables contained within the box and place them within a bowl.

Within

The class of items within the salad, within the bowl, is vegetables. Although not present, radishes, of the same class, are included.

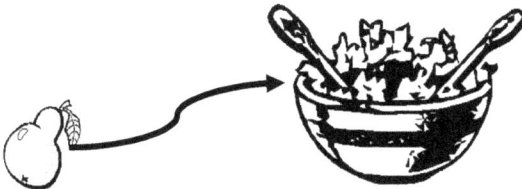

If pears are included within the salad and within the bowl, then a different class of food is within.

This is the concept of jurisdiction as applied to law. This concept also applies to the federal income tax. The concept of being within and without is simple and critical. The discernment of legal terms and their meanings and the application of tax law are complicated. Laws are written beyond the comprehension of those with the highest levels of education and intellect. Yet, if we understand the *within* and *without* concept, we will understand tax law.

Since the tax laws *may* apply to you, the obvious question must be asked: Am I within or without? Am I included or excluded? Regardless of any given interpretation of any statute, regulation, or court ruling, it is essential to know our status and whether or not we are within a given jurisdiction. For example, Title 28 of the United States Code, Section 1746, deals with unsworn declarations. The language explains two ways to sign: *without the United States or within the United States*.

> Title 28 – Judiciary and Judicial Procedure
> Part V Procedure, Chapter 115 Evidence
> **1746. Unsworn declarations under penalty of perjury**
> Wherever, under any law of the United States or under any rule, regulation, order, or requirement made pursuant to law, any matter is required or permitted to be supported, evidenced, established, or proved by the sworn declaration, verification, certificate, statement, oath, or affidavit, in writing of the person making the same (other than a deposition, or an oath required to be taken before a specified official other than a notary public), such matter may, with like force and effect, be supported, evidenced, established or proved by the unsworn declaration, certificate, verification, or statement, in writing of such

person which is subscribed by him, as true under penalty of perjury, and dated, in substantially the following form:

(1)   If executed **without the United States**: "I declare (or certify, verify, or state) under penalty of perjury under the laws of the United States of America that the foregoing is true and correct. Executed on (date). Signature."

(2)   If executed **within the United States**, its territories, possessions, or commonwealths: "I declare (or certify, verify, or state) under penalty of perjury under the laws of the United States of America that the foregoing is true and correct. Executed on (date). Signature."

Note the statute qualifies what is *within* the *United States*— territories, possessions, or commonwealths. Does the term *United States* in section 1746 *include* the 50 States? If so, is the law clear? The Supreme Court stated:

In the case of doubt, they [revenue laws] are construed most strongly against the government, and in favor of the citizen. *Gould v Gould, 245 US 151 (1917)* [brackets added]

Citizens must be able to know the law; anything less than clear language is confusing. We should know if we are *within or without the United States*. If the language is obscure, we should ask if the statute is written with the intent to deceive.

There are many definitions for the term *United States* which do not mean what we generally accept. Depending upon how *United States* is used in any given code section, the meaning will change. We should not be surprised of various meanings for other legal terms that are inconsistent with an ordinary use. Here is an example. The legal term *person* does not have the same meaning as commonly used. This brings us back to the concept of *within and without*. Under 1746, we know the United States *includes territories, possessions, and commonwealths. Who is a person?*

Territories
possessions
commonwealths

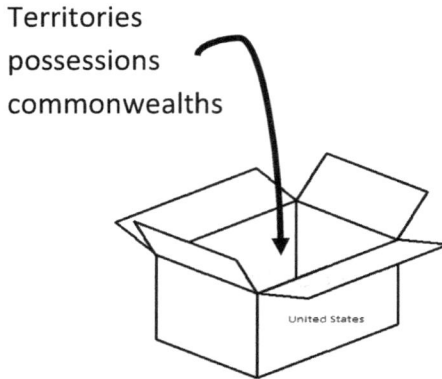

United States

This list is *the class within the United States*, just as bananas, apples, oranges, peaches, and grapes represent a class within a bowl. We know the 50 States, a separate class, is not included. The 50 States are not *within the United States*, just as the pears were *without* the salad until placed within.

Are we included or excluded? Are we within or without the United States when we sign a declaration in accord with 28 USC 1746? The answer may not be obvious. First, if we don't know the term *United States* means *territories, possessions, or commonwealths*, we accept our common and uninformed understanding of the legal term and unknowingly include ourselves within the *United States*. Yet, if we know United States includes a limited class, we understand that we are excluded.

This is a vital point. If we have no idea we are *without* the *United States* and we include ourselves *within*, we *are within* the *United States* just as broccoli is eventually placed within the bowl of fruit, an item within a separate class of food that did not belong and was included by broccoli's *permission*. The concept of being granted permission has significance. We will learn that we unknowingly entered *within the United States* by permission and, as a result, became liable for the federal income tax.

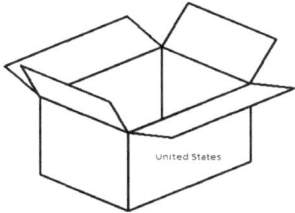

This is the *United States*.

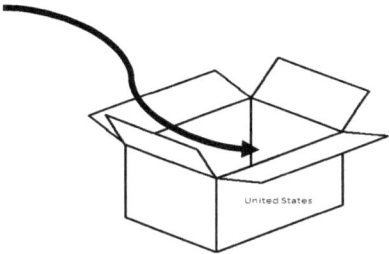

Anything or anyone inside the *United States* is within.

State Citizens   people in foreign countries

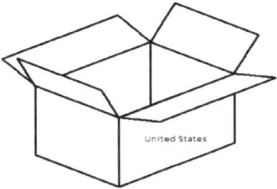

Those outside of the *United States* are without.

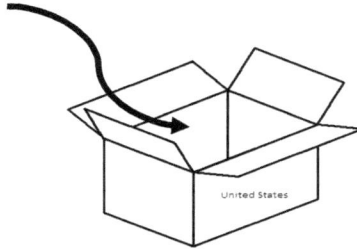

Without

If one is *within the United States*, he is without the jurisdiction of his State, even if only for a given purpose.

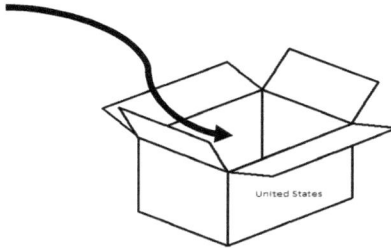

Within

The *class within the United States* and subject to the income tax is defined by legal terms in the tax code: "person," "individual," "U.S. person," "taxpayer," "resident," and "nonresident alien."

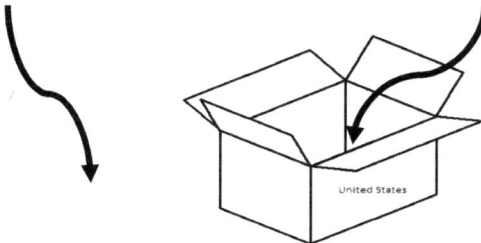

Without   Within

If within the *United States*, is one a *U.S person* liable for the tax?

Ask the obvious question. How does an American go from being without to within the United States for the income tax?

Within

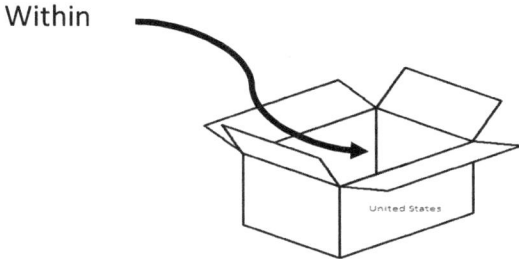

In order to answer this query, we must understand the relation of the *United States* to the 50 States of the Union.

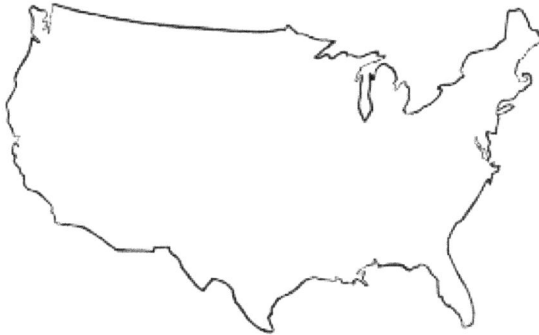

This is the united States of America, the 50 States.

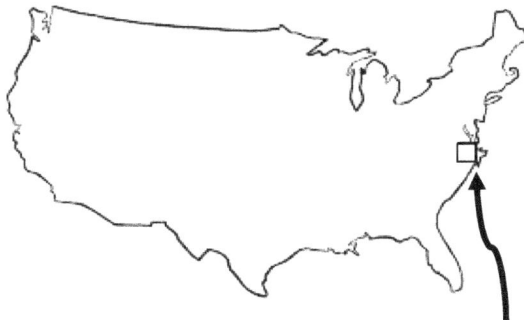

This is the *United States* Government in Washington, D.C.

The *United States* is a federal territory with its own citizens.

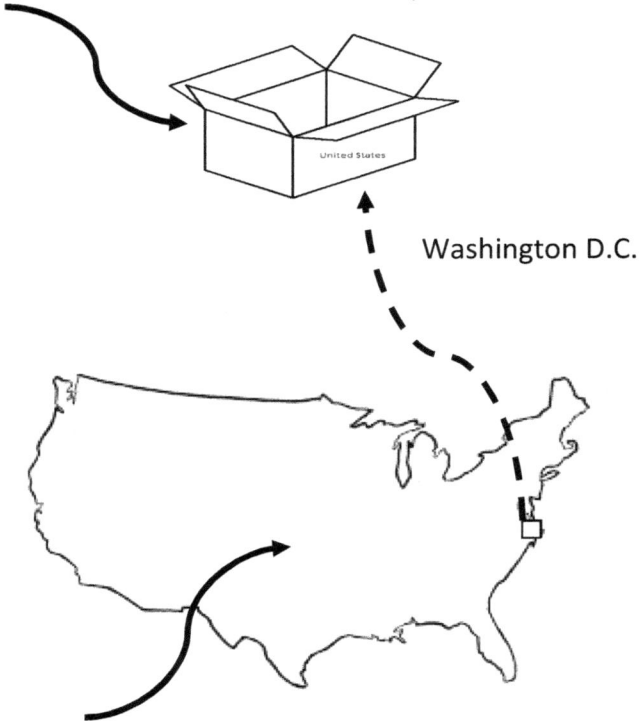

Washington D.C.

The united States of America has its own Citizens.

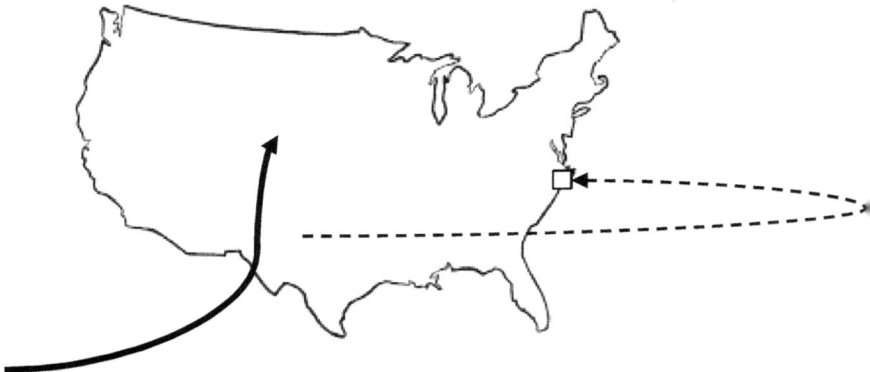

Americans are without the *united States* until and unless they enter within the jurisdiction of the United States.

Warning: As you examine the content of this book, pay particular attention to concepts which will unfold. For example, you will encounter the term "parens patriae." Consider this definition:

> Parens Patriae
>
> [Latin, Parent of the country.] A doctrine that grants the inherent power and authority of the state to protect persons who are legally unable to act on their own behalf.[6]

You will eventually see this term within this book. Stop at that point and weigh the complete context and then consider how the federal government views you. Your perspective should be forever altered.

---

[6] http://legal-dictionary.thefreedictionary.com/parens+patriae

Deceit

In 1964, Congress granted President Johnson the authority to intervene militarily in Vietnam. This congressional resolution was predicated upon an August 4th attack by the North Vietnamese on U. S. naval vessels in the Gulf of Tonkin. However, such hostile aggression never occurred. As revealed in a declassified National Security Agency (NSA) document, written by Robert Hanyok,[7] the allegation was not true. With the declassification and release of this document, the NSA was

> fearful that [declassification] might prompt uncomfortable comparisons with the flawed intelligence used to justify the war in Iraq.[8]

In 2002, President Bush asserted Iraq's leader, Saddam Hussein, acquired "yellowcake uranium."[9] Bush used this *intelligence*, also a falsehood, as justification to invade Iraq. Naturally, the NSA wanted to delay full disclosure of a dated armed conflict (Vietnam) which would bring greater scrutiny on another. The government does not want a refutation of its disinformation (notice the absence of the word *intelligence*), especially when it intends to deceive.

When event after event is marked with an all-too-common signature—corruption—such deceit leads to our greater understanding. For example, the U. S. Government successfully cracked the Japanese code prior to the attack on Pearl Harbor.[10] Did the government have foreknowledge, credible intelligence, of a Japanese assault on America? With Pearl Harbor, Vietnam, and

---

[7] http://nsarchive.gwu.edu/NSAEBB/NSAEBB132/relea00012.pdf
[8] http://www.nytimes.com/2005/10/31/politics/vietnam-study-castingdoubts-remains-secret.html
[9] https://en.wikipedia.org/wiki/Niger_uranium_forgeriesfrom Niger
[10] http://www.independent.org/newsroom/article.asp?id=408

Iraq, is there a pattern? The conclusion becomes rather obvious. The Government cannot and should not be trusted.

With such examples, video documentaries like the one produced by "Loose Change,"[11] a fully vetted examination of the 9-11 attacks, become even more credible. Such research should cause us to seek what is incongruent with government decisions, declarations, and actions. Many Americans know the real cause and circumstances of 9-11 are not as claimed by the United States Government, just as the infamous *Patriot Act*, passed in support of the *War on Terror*, is held suspect.

With the foregoing examples, the motives and practices of the Government are profound and troubling. In fact, introducing a declassified NSA document about the contrived Gulf of Tonkin incident in a book about tax law may not be strange after all. This declassified document is relevant for one salient reason. The United States Government handles tax related issues in the same deceptive manner. There is a common theme with respect to the internal culture of the *United States* ruling bureaucracy. Read an excerpt of the NSA document and question whether we should trust the government and its enforcement of laws.

---

[11] https://www.youtube.com/watch?v=DXRDq9nKJ0U

(U) Skunks, Bogies, Silent Hounds, and the Flying Fish: The Gulf of Tonkin Mystery, 2-4 August 1964

ROBERT J. HANYOK

(C//SI) The Gulf of Tonkin incidents of 2 to 4 August 1964 have come to loom over the subsequent American engagement in Indochina. The incidents, principally the second one of 4 August, led to the approval of the Gulf of Tonkin Resolution by the U.S. Congress, which handed President Johnson the carte blanche charter he had wanted for future intervention in Southeast Asia. From this point on, the American policy and programs would dominate the course of the Indochina War. At the height of the American involvement, over a half million U.S. soldiers, sailors, airmen, and marines would be stationed there. The war would spread across the border into Cambodia and escalate in Laos. Thailand assumed a greater importance as a base for supporting the military effort, especially for the air war, but also for SIGINT purposes of intercept and direction finding.

(U) At the time, the Gulf of Tonkin incidents of August were not quite so controversial. According to the Johnson administration, the issue of the attacks was pretty much cut and dried. As the administration explained, our ships had been in international waters – anywhere from fifty to eighty miles from the DRV coastline by some calculations, during the alleged second attack – and were attacked twice, even though they were innocent of any bellicose gestures directed at North Vietnam. Secretary of Defense Robert McNamara had assured the Senate that there had been no connection between what the U.S. Navy was doing and any aggressive operations by the South Vietnamese.[1] Washington claimed that the United States had to defend itself and guarantee freedom of navigation on the high seas.

(U) However, within the government, the events of 4 August were never that clear. Even as the last flare fizzled in the dark waters of the South China Sea on that August night, there were conflicting narratives and interpretations of what had happened. James Stockdale, then a navy pilot at the scene, who had "the best seat in the house from which to detect boats," saw nothing. "No boats," he would later write, "no boat wakes, no ricochets off boats, no boat impacts, no torpedo wakes – nothing but black sea and American firepower."[2] The commander of the *Maddox* task force, Captain John J. Herrick, was not entirely certain what had transpired. (Captain Herrick actually was the commander of the destroyer division to which the *Maddox* belonged. For this mission, he was aboard as the on-site commander.) Hours after the incident, he would radio the Commander-in-Chief, Pacific (CINCPAC) telling them that he was doubtful of many aspects of the "attack."

(U) It would be years before any evidence that an attack had not happened finally emerged in the public domain, and even then, most reluctantly. Yet, remarkably, some of the major participants in the events still maintained that the Gulf of Tonkin incident had occurred just as it had been originally reported. Secretary of Defense Robert McNamara, in his memoirs *In Retrospect*, considered the overall evidence for an attack still convincing.[3] The U.S. Navy's history of the Vietnam conflict, written by Edward J. Marolda and Oscar P. Fitzgerald (hereafter referred to as the "Marolda-Fitzgerald history"), reported that the evidence for the second attack, especially from intelligence, including a small amount of SIGINT, was considered conclusive.[4]

Derived From: NSA/CSSM 123-2
24 February 1998
Declassify On: X1

16

(U) The public literature on the Gulf of Tonkin for years has been overwhelmingly skeptical about the 4 August battle. Articles that appeared in magazines within a few years illustrated the general inconsistency in the descriptions of the incident of 4 August by simply using the conflicting testimony from the officers and crews of both ships. The first major critical volume was Joseph Goulden's *Truth Is the First Casualty*, published in 1969. The most complete work to date is Edwin Moise's *Tonkin Gulf and the Escalation of the Vietnam War*. Moise's work has the dual advantage of using some Vietnamese sources, as well as small portions of a few SIGINT reports released to the author under a Freedom of Information Act request. Yet, even what few scraps he received from NSA were enough to raise serious questions about the validity of the SIGINT reports cited by the administration which related to the 4 August incident.[5]

(S//SI) The issue of whether the available SIGINT "proved" that there had been a second attack has been argued for years. In 1968, Robert McNamara testified before Senator William Fulbright's Foreign Relations Committee's hearings on the Gulf of Tonkin that the supporting signals intelligence was "unimpeachable." On the other hand, in 1972 the deputy director of NSA, Louis Tordella, was quoted as saying that the 4 August intercepts pertained to the 2 August attacks. In a 1975 article in the NSA magazine *Cryptolog*, the Gulf of Tonkin incident was retold, but the SIGINT for the night of August 4 was not mentioned, except for the "military operations" intercept, and even then without comment.[6] The Navy's history of the Vietnam War would misconstrue the SIGINT (disguised as unsourced "intelligence") associating portions of two critical intercepts and implying a connection in the evidence where none could be established.[7]

(C//SI) Except for the sizable collection of SIGINT material within NSA, and a much smaller amount from the archives of the Naval Security Group (which essentially duplicates portions of

the NSA holdings), almost all relevant material relating to the Gulf of Tonkin incidents has been released. Although the questions about what happened in the Gulf of Tonkin on the night of 4 August have been fairly well answered by the evidence from all of the other sources – radar, sonar, eyewitness, and archival – the SIGINT version needs to be told. This is because of the critical role that SIGINT played in defining the second attack in the minds of Johnson administration officials. Without the signals intelligence information, the administration had only the confused and conflicting testimony and evidence of the men and equipment involved in the incident. It is difficult to imagine the 5 August retaliatory air strikes against North Vietnamese naval bases and installations being ordered without the SIGINT "evidence."[8] Therefore, it is necessary to recount in some detail what signals intelligence reported.

(S//SI) For the first time ever, what will be presented in the following narrative is the *complete* SIGINT version of what happened in the Gulf of Tonkin between 2 and 4 August 1964. Until now, the NSA has officially maintained that the second incident of 4 August occurred. This position was established in the initial SIGINT reports of 4 August and sustained through a series of summary reports issued shortly after the crisis. In October 1964, a classified chronology of events for 2 to 4 August in the Gulf of Tonkin was published by NSA which furthered the contention that the second attack had occurred.

(S//SI) In maintaining the official version of the attack, the NSA made use of surprisingly few published SIGINT reports – fifteen in all. The research behind the new version which follows is based on the discovery of an enormous amount of never-before-used SIGINT material. This included 122 relevant SIGINT products, along with watch center notes, oral history interviews, and messages among the various SIGINT and military command centers involved in the Gulf of Tonkin incidents. Naturally, this flood of new information changed dramatically the story of that night

17

of 4/5 August. The most important element is that it is now known what the North Vietnamese Navy was doing that night. And with this information a nearly complete story finally can be told.

(S//SI) Two startling findings emerged from the new research. First, it is not simply that there is a different story as to what happened; it is that *no attack* happened that night. Through a compound of analytic errors and an unwillingness to consider contrary evidence, American SIGINT elements in the region and at NSA HQs reported Hanoi's plans to attack the two ships of the Desoto patrol. Further analytic errors and an obscuring of other information led to publication of more "evidence." In truth, Hanoi's navy was engaged in nothing that night but the salvage of two of the boats damaged on 2 August.

(S//SI) The second finding pertains to the handling of the SIGINT material related to the Gulf of Tonkin by individuals at NSA. Beginning with the period of the crisis in early August, into the days of the immediate aftermath, and continuing into October 1964, SIGINT information was presented in such a manner as to preclude responsible decisionmakers in the Johnson administration from having the complete and objective narrative of events of 4 August 1964. Instead, only SIGINT that supported the claim that the communists had attacked the two destroyers was given to administration officials.

(S//SI) This mishandling of the SIGINT was not done in a manner that can be construed as conspiratorial, that is, with manufactured evidence and collusion at all levels. Rather, the objective of these individuals was to support the Navy's claim that the Desoto patrol had been deliberately attacked by the North Vietnamese. Yet, in order to substantiate that claim, all of the relevant SIGINT could not be provided to the White House and the Defense and intelligence officials. The conclusion that would be drawn from a review of all SIGINT evidence would have been that the North Vietnamese not only did not

attack, but were uncertain as to the location of the ships.

(S//SI) Instead, three things occurred with the SIGINT. First of all, the overwhelming portion of the SIGINT relevant to 4 August was kept out of the post-attack summary reports and the final report written in October 1964. The withheld information constituted nearly 90 percent of all available SIGINT. This information revealed the actual activities of the North Vietnamese on the night of 4 August that included salvage operations of the two torpedo boats damaged on 2 August, and coastal patrols by a small number of DRV craft. As will be demonstrated later in this chapter, the handful of SIGINT reports which suggested that an attack had occurred contained severe analytic errors, unexplained translation changes, and the conjunction of two unrelated messages into one translation. This latter product would become the Johnson administration's main proof of the 4 August attack.

(S//SI) Second, there were instances in which specious supporting SIGINT evidence was inserted into NSA summary reports issued shortly after the Gulf of Tonkin incidents. This SIGINT was not manufactured. Instead, it consisted of fragments of legitimate intercept lifted out of its context and inserted into the summary reports to support the contention of a premeditated North Vietnamese attack on 4 August. The sources of these fragments were not even referenced in the summaries. It took extensive research before the original reports containing these items could be identified.

(S//SI) Finally, there is the unexplained disappearance of vital decrypted Vietnamese text of the translation that was the basis of the administration's most important evidence – the so-called Vietnamese after-action report of late 4 August. The loss of the text is important because the SIGINT record shows that there were critical differences in the English translations of it issued both by the navy intercept site in the Philippines and

In light of the Gulf of Tonkin intelligence, recent NSA spying scandals involving the collection of data against Americans, and the admission that the NSA spies on its allies[12] (Eric Snowden and Julian Assange), we should not be surprised that the Government deceives Americans routinely and by design. To illustrate, did you know the federal income tax is an "excise" tax, which means it is an "indirect" tax and, therefore, "voluntary" only the first time the tax return is filed? Once a return is submitted, the IRS expects (demands) compliance every year thereafter. What would you think if elected officials refused to answer specific questions about tax laws? You may learn the Government approaches tax issues no differently than any covert operation, with denials, disinformation, and subterfuge. Note the enclosed memorandum from former President Barack Hussein Obama.[13]

---

[12] http://www.nytimes.com/2013/12/21/world/nsa-dragnet-included-allies-aid-groups-and-business-elite.html

[13] https://en.wikisource.org/wiki/Memorandum_of_January_20,_2010 (https://www.gpo.gov/fdsys/pkg/FR-2010-01-25/pdf/2010-1561.pdf)

Memorandum of January 20, 2010 *by Barack Obama*
Addressing Tax Delinquency by Government Contractor

Issued on 22 January 2010. *Federal Register* page and date: 75 FR 3979, January 25, 2010

MEMORANDUM FOR THE HEADS OF EXECUTIVE DEPARTMENTS AND AGENCIES

SUBJECT: Addressing Tax Delinquency by Government Contractors

The Federal Government pays more than half a trillion dollars a year to contractors and has an important obligation to protect American taxpayer money and the integrity of the Federal acquisition process. Yet reports by the Government Accountability Office (GAO) state that Federal contracts are awarded to tens of thousands of companies with serious tax delinquencies. The total amount in unpaid taxes owed by these contracting companies is estimated to be more than $5 billion.

Too often, Federal contracting officials do not have the most basic information they need to make informed judgments about whether a company trying to win a Federal contract is delinquent in paying its taxes. We need to give our contracting officials the tools they need to protect taxpayer dollars.

Accordingly, I hereby direct the Commissioner of Internal Revenue (Commissioner) to direct a review of certifications of non-delinquency in taxes that companies bidding for Federal contracts are required to submit pursuant to a 2008 amendment to the Federal Acquisition Regulation. I further direct that the Commissioner report to me within 90 days on the overall accuracy of contractors' certifications.

I also direct the Director of the Office of Management and Budget, working with the Secretary of the Treasury and other agency heads, to evaluate practices of contracting officers and debarring officials in response to contractors' certifications of serious tax delinquencies and to provide me, within 90 days, recommendations on process improvements to ensure these contractors are not awarded new contracts, including a plan to make contractor certifications available in a Government-wide database, as is already being done with other information on contractors.

Executive departments and agencies shall carry out the provisions of this memorandum to the extent permitted by law. This memorandum is not intended to, and does not, create any right or benefit, substantive or procedural, enforceable at law or in equity by any party against the United States, its departments, agencies, or entities, its officers, employees, or agents, or any other person.

The Director of the Office of Management and Budget is hereby authorized and directed to publish this memorandum in the **Federal Register**.

BARACK OBAMA

THE WHITE HOUSE,
WASHINGTON, January 22, 2010.

20

As the United States Government pursues and prosecutes a handful of Americans who have with the intent to comply with the *correct* application of the income tax law, Obama admits to tens of thousands of contractors "with serious tax delinquencies." The contractors are *U.S. persons* with a federal status or privilege who willfully failed to file federal income tax returns—a crime. Then there are 300,000 federal employees, active and retired, who are delinquent with their federal taxes.[14] Why doesn't the IRS investigate these *individuals* (as legally defined) as criminals?

Federal contractors and employees—whether corporations or human beings—are *persons, individuals, and taxpayers* within the *United States*. They are legally liable for the income tax. Yet, the Government excuses delinquent taxpayers while it imprisons innocent Americans who are *without* congressional taxing power. Do government officials enforce laws to maintain a level of fear and compliance among an unsuspecting people? This strategy prevents a revolution within the minds and hearts of the people.

Let's begin a journey which will compel us to ask if we are within one jurisdiction or another. This query is important, as the Federal Government may only exercise authority over whom and what are within its domain. Is it possible we were or are outside federal jurisdiction? This question requires us to consider whether we have unwittingly placed ourselves within federal jurisdiction and become liable for the income tax. Note,

> The Social Security Act **does not require a person to have a Social Security number** (SSN) **to live or work in the United States**, nor does it require an SSN simply for the purpose of having one. Letter from *Charles Mullen, Associate Commissioner, SSA, Office of Public Inquiries (1948)*

---

[14] (http://www.pbs.org/newshour/rundown/irs-says-305000-federal-workers-retirees-owe-3-5-billion-back-taxes/)

A social security number is generally identified in the records and database of the Internal Revenue Service as belonging to a ***U.S. citizen or resident alien individual. A person may establish a different status for the number by providing proof of foreign status with the Internal Revenue Service*** under such procedures as the Internal Revenue Service shall prescribe, including the use of a form as the Internal Revenue Service may specify. ***Upon accepting an individual as a nonresident alien individual, the Internal Revenue Service will assign this status to the individual's social security number***. *26 CFR 301.6109-1(g)(1)(i)*

Now consider the text in 26 USC 6013(g) and (h).

(g) ELECTION TO TREAT NONRESIDENT ALIEN INDIVIDUAL AS RESIDENT OF THE UNITED STATES

(1) IN GENERAL. A **nonresident alien individual** with respect to whom this subsection is in effect for the taxable year **shall be treated as a resident of the United States** -

(4) TERMINATION OF ELECTION. An election under this subsection shall terminate at the earliest of the following times:
(A) Revocation by taxpayers
If either taxpayer revokes the election, as of the first taxable year for which the last day prescribed by law for filing the return of tax under chapter 1 has not yet occurred.

(h) JOINT RETURN, ETC., FOR YEAR IN WHICH NONRESIDENT ALIEN BECOMES RESIDENT of UNITED STATES
(1) IN GENERAL. If-
(A)

any individual is a nonresident alien individual at the beginning of any taxable year **but is a resident of the United States** at the close of such taxable year,

For purposes of the federal income tax, *nonresidents*—as in those not resident to the *United States*—may be classified as residents upon election. Nonresidents may elect not to be classified as *residents*. It should be transparent that not all people are liable for the federal income tax. Are the 10,000 contractors *resident aliens* subject to the tax code? Are there *nonresidents* who are *without* the scope of the tax code?

Legal terms and their meanings are not the same as everyday common usage. The legal world is driven by terms and definitions which accomplish specific objectives. The fact that we are not aware of the meanings of legal terms or the intent of the code is problematic. Our ignorance is used to our detriment. For this reason, we should question who we are in the context of any given law. Is a *resident alien*, who must be a *U.S. person, person, individual, taxpayer*, or some other federal classification, liable for the federal income tax? Is a *nonresident without the United States* liable for the income tax? Isn't it obvious we should question what we believe to be true?

Understanding the Law

Consider the possibility that:

a)   We don't know what we do not know.

b)   What we do *know* is not necessarily the truth.

c)   Our perceptions and opinions are reality.

d)   We are often too comfortable and apathetic to understand what is credible.

e)   We often disbelieve what is true and are too fearful to reject what is false.

It is often said if one wishes to learn, he should do as he does with an onion—peel back another layer. Supposedly the next layer reflects or contains greater knowledge and leads to understanding. This analogy is perfect for a scientist with the intent to explore from a perspective of not knowing. However, aside from a probative endeavor, the premise of the onion analogy is flawed.

If we already *know* what we believe to be true, even if it is false, any added *knowledge* would be, potentially, equally false. We need only weigh any issue. To substantiate this conclusion, consider the impact of the Copernican Theory. Before Copernicus explored, before he peeled layers which revealed greater insight, people believed the earth was the center of the universe. This notion was accepted as truth and rarely questioned. Notably, *information* from the governing authority at the time, the Catholic Church, which dictated the prominence of the earth within the universe, was received as equally valid. Yet, the proposition was never credible. If we apply the five foregoing observations, we see how each is relevant.

a)   People did not know that they did not know the sun was the center of the universe.

b)   What people knew of the earth and its relationship with the universe was false.

c)   The perception people had about the universe, although false, was their reality.

d)   People accepted what they knew to be true, if only because they were too comfortable, apathetic, or fearful to understand otherwise.

e)   People did not believe the actual truth and, thus, did not counter the prevailing ideology and power of the Catholic Church, which decreed an official theory.

The Copernican Theory supports the notion that the onion analogy is perfect for scientific or mathematical research and misapplied to what is already *known*. Whether or not we recognize this dynamic, it is a practical reality. One may peel and be no closer to the truth and any final conclusion would be meritless. Regardless of the issue, we default to a limited perspective. The context of our understanding is finite. It would be prudent to ask how and why we arrive at any determination.

As with a sixth-grade student, our understanding is confined to what we know. With the above five observations as a frame of reference, let's posit that, based upon what we understand, we are not outside the onion, but, rather, we are at the center. The center of the onion is very small, hard, and dense. It is not able to be peeled. This is where we exist. The core represents what we *know* as *truth*. Unless we explore outwardly, we will understand no more than what we permit. If we fail to ask questions, our growth will remain shallow and our perspective static. This mindset reflects a micro view and a refusal to venture into the macro.

Hopefully we can see the way out, the path to truth, is away from the center of the onion. Since we cannot peel from the inside, we must claw through the inner most layers to reach the exterior. With each layer, we dispel false notions, dispense with disbelief and avail ourselves to truth.

Let's test this supposition as it relates to the realm of law. Most Americans believe the term *United States* means the 50 states and nothing more. This is a limited perspective and incorrect and reflects our small and uninformed view—the center of the onion. If we were not at the center of the onion, rather, if we were outside and peeled layers based upon the wrong definition of *United States*—the only definition we knew—the law would be no more correctly understood. If we learn *United States* means only the executive, legislative, and judicial branches of the federal government, we might readily reject this definition. Such is the power of disbelief. This is no different than how the Copernican Theory was received. Note:

a)   We do not know that we do not know *United States* means something contrary to our understanding.

b)   If only for our definition of *United States*, what we know of the law is either false or incomplete.

c)   Our perceptions and opinions about the law, although false, are a reality.

d)   What we *know* of *truth* is only because we are too comfortable or apathetic to understand anything else.

e)   We disbelieve the actual truth because we are too fearful to counter our perception or misunderstanding.

Those who are not willing to comprehend the correct definition of *United States* will continue as before. They will remain comfortable within their own ignorance, within the hard and dense place—the center of the onion. Those who understand *United States* means something more than the readily accepted definition may venture beyond their limitations. They may push the confines of what they know and enter the outer layers. Some will reach the third, fourth, and fifth layers and become more enlightened. Even fewer people will reach the exterior.

We arrive at a grave dilemma. Few people have context of a given topic, whether the Gulf of Tonkin, 9-11, the definition of *United States,* or tax law. Given the inherent complexity of the tax code, few reach a grounded understanding of this controversial topic. Few understand until and unless they allow for insight which would otherwise be dismissed.

How do we resolve this problem? Let's consider a simple solution. There are facts which must be accepted as fundamental. If we accept what others have established, if we understand that they have pierced through the exterior of the onion and into the realm of truth, we may increase our knowledge. We benefit from the suspension of our own disbelief. It is then that we understand how and why Americans become *U.S. persons* and *U.S. citizens* liable for the federal income tax and how Americans may keep themselves *without* the United States or extract themselves from federal jurisdiction.

We must consider what is unthinkable. What we believe about the federal income tax is not true. This is pivotal. We should defeat any compunction to peel layers which lead to greater lies. Rather, we should breach into knowledge that is outside, but within our reach. Those who have delved into federal tax law and acquired full context are not saddled by the five observations. As with the few who agreed with Copernicus, those daring enough to depart from the official view of the earth's supposed prominence, we may know the truth about the income tax. Consider that:

a)   We do not know that we do not know the federal income tax is an excise tax which one is obligated to pay upon the acceptance of a federal privilege or status.

b)   What we know about the income tax law is false.

c)   Our perceptions and opinions about the federal income tax law, although false, are a reality.

d)   We accept what we know about tax law as true if only because we are too comfortable or apathetic to understand truth.

e)   We disbelieve truth or are too fearful to counter falsehoods, which is disinformation enforced by the government.

Clearly, Americans have and would have serious reservations negotiating the proper context of tax law. It is safer to accept the lie and remain at the center of the onion.

Let's explore outer layers of difficult concepts. The federal tax code, regulations, and court cases are more complex than a sixth-grade education and beyond the level of those with doctoral degrees. So, the next few pages will serve as a primer concerning fundamentals of the federal income tax law. We will establish:

- basic concepts which are critical to comprehend what is rather complex;
- facts about federal jurisdiction and tax law.

1)   The 50 (several States) are "free and independent States"[15] known as the united States of America. While we often refer to the 50 States as the *United States*, a rather casual everyday expression, in law *United States* means something different.

2)   The legal term *United States* is defined as Washington, D.C., Guam, Puerto Rico, the Virgin Islands, federal territories, military posts, naval bases, forts, forests, and property unique to the

---

[15] The Declaration of Independence

Federal Government. Such places and property are outside of and not a part of the 50 States of the Union.

3)   The "Constitution of the United States of America" created the Federal Government—the *United States*. The Constitution limits the authority of the *United States* to eighteen powers under Article 1, Section 8, powers granted by the States.

4)   The *United States* has unlimited authority and jurisdiction over its own territory, property, and persons. However, it has limited jurisdiction with respect to the 50 States.

5)   Under the Constitution, the *United States*—the Federal Government—may tax by direct and indirect means.

> The Congress shall have Power To lay and collect Taxes, Duties, Imposts and Excises, to pay the Debts and provide for the common Defence and general Welfare of the United States; but all Duties, Imposts and Excises shall be uniform throughout the United States; *Article I, Section 8, Clause 1*

> Representatives and direct Taxes shall be apportioned among the several States which may be included within this Union, according to their respective Numbers, which shall be determined by adding to the whole Number of free Persons, including those bound to Service for a Term of Years, and excluding Indians not taxed, three fifths of all other Persons. *Article I, Section 2, Clause 3*

> No Capitation, or other direct, Tax shall be laid, unless in Proportion to the Census or Enumeration herein before directed to be taken. *Article I, Section 9, Clauses 3*

6)   Since the *United States* cannot directly tax the people or their property, the *United States* must "apportion" taxes by proportionately allocating the amount of the total tax to each State based on its percentage of the national population.

7)   The *United States* may impose indirect taxes. Indirect taxes must be the same across the country. Indirect taxes are *voluntary*. When Americans voluntarily enter into or engage the activity for which there is an indirect tax, it must be paid. Gasoline has an indirect tax which must be paid when voluntarily purchased.

8)   Indirect taxes are *excises*. Excises are assessed against "commodities," "certain occupations," and "privileges."[16]

9)   The federal *income* tax is an indirect or excise tax, which makes it voluntary.

10)   The definition of *income*, as settled by the United States Supreme Court, means "profit" or "gain."[17] It is also the amount upon which an excise is assessed for a privilege.

11)   The earnings of Americans are not *wages* as legally defined in the tax code until Americans accept a federal privilege or status. *Wages* is a legal term used with a specific intent.

12)   Americans have an unalienable and natural right to labor. Labor is a man's property which the United States Government may not tax directly. The United States Government cannot tax a man's earnings as *wages* until he accepts a federal occupation,

---

[16] Flint v Stone Tracy, 220 US 107 (1911)]
[17] [Eisner v Macomber, 348 US 426 (1955)

privilege, or status. Conversely, a man's earnings are property equally exchanged for other property that is labor. There is no *profit or gain* (income) from this exchange.

13)   In 1862, Congress enacted the first federal income tax on *employment*. Those who worked for the United States were *employees* within the jurisdiction of federal taxing authority. Those who voluntarily accepted the *privilege* of working for the government were obligated to pay the *income* tax upon *wages*.

14)   The federal United States enacted the Social Security Act in 1935, a federal program for the *United States* and its territories and possessions. The 48 States at the time could choose to participate and terminate their involvement with this insurance scheme. Participation was not and is not mandatory for Americans within the 50 States.

15)   In 1937, the Supreme Court determined *employers* were subject to an indirect tax for the benefit/privilege of *employing employees*. The Supreme Court considered the "relation of employment" [18] as excisable. However, *employers, employees, and employment* are legal terms with specific definitions. These terms had nothing to do with private businesses in the 48 States at the time.

16)   The Social Security scheme is a privilege or benefit subject to *excise* by *indirect* tax. Those who voluntarily accept this benefit and subsequent federal status are subject to an excise upon *wages* earned and paid. As such, they are **within** the United States and deemed to be *employers and employees*.

---

[18] Charles C Steward Machine v Davis and Helvering v Davis

17) Within the tax code, the terms *employer and employee* are limited to the *United States*. When businesses and Americans complete tax forms, they enter within federal jurisdiction under the "relation of employment" as *employers or employees.*

> (c) Services performed **outside the United States** – (1) In general. Except as provided in paragraphs (c)(2) and (3) of this section, **services performed outside [without] the United States do not constitute employment**. *26 USC, Part 31-Employment Taxes and Collection of Income Tax at Source, Subpart B-Federal Insurance Contributions Act, 31.3121(b)-3 Employment; services performed after 1954*

18) Private business owner and Americans are deceived and misinformed. Consequently, they complete and submit federal employment tax forms such as W-2s and W-4s. Once voluntarily tendered, the *presumption* is that business owners are employers and Americans are employees *within the United States.* Yet, note:

> **Private employers**, states, and political subdivisions are not required to enter into payroll deduction agreements. Taxpayers should determine whether their employers will accept and process executed agreements before agreements are submitted for approval or finalized. *Internal Revenue Manual, Section 5.14.10.2 (09-30-2004), Payroll Deduction Agreements*

19) Regrettably, Americans treat the terms *employer and employee* the same as they treat the terms *income* and *United States*. They are used in a casual manner rather than with the legal significance applied in the 1862 income tax law and the

current tax code, which is applicable to federal employees who work for or contract with the U. S.

20)   When Americans voluntarily submit their first tax return, they create prima facie evidence that they are federal taxpayers with income (wages) subject to indirect tax. The United States and IRS expect tax returns to be filed annually thereafter.

21)   The collection of income taxes (indirect excises) is legal, lawful, and constitutional. The United States is simply collecting the tax from those who voluntarily enter the jurisdiction of the *United States* upon acceptance of a federal privilege or status.

22)   Americans unknowingly enter the federal social security scheme and "relation of employment" if only because parents, businesses, schools, and officials state that compliance is required. This is disinformation. Americans become liable for the federal income tax when they accept federal privileges, document themselves as federal employees, and designate themselves with a federal status within the *United States*.

23)   The *income* tax—a tax on *income*—has a limited scope within a limited jurisdiction. Thus, according to the legal terms of the tax code, Americans become *taxpayers, persons, United States persons, and employees*—legal terms with limited application.

24)   Those who either do not accept or reject federal benefits, privileges, or classifications are not involved in a federally excisable obligation and, as a result, cannot be within the scope of federal tax law. Americans who accept such federal designations are *within the United States* for federal income tax purposes.

25)   To correct the presumption of a tax liability, one must rebut that he is a *taxpayer* within congressional taxing power.

No official within the federal United States Government will explain the tax code or answer basic questions. Many officials do not understand the tax code. This is by design. Those who have a correct understanding have the express intent to perpetuate a deceptive application of the law.

As difficult as this information may be to accept, consider that our disbelief does not make the truth any less credible. If we allow any of the five observations to inhibit our thinking, so be it. However, we should not discount what others now understand. Just as we give credence to a heart surgeon or an astrophysicist for what they know, we should recognize the painstaking efforts of those who comprehend an accurate assessment of tax law.

The Value of Language

The existence, survival, and success of humanity are predicated upon language. The ability to communicate with grunts and signals, verbally, or with the written word is essential.

Language, as a tool, serves a purpose. That purpose, for good or harm, is achieved when an intent or objective is communicated and understood. As a matter of course, one communicates and another receives what is communicated. The actual message may be clear or confused. Even if the message is clear, the person interpreting the meaning may arrive at a flawed understanding. If the message is not transparent from the outset, the intent of the message will not likely be known.

Consider communication in a foreign language. If one does not know the language, the message will remain unknown. If conveyed by someone who knows the language, the interpretation by the translator or the understanding of the recipient may not be exact. While language may be precise, it is quite often not received as such.

The import of this explanation is that the realm of *law*, often referred to as the justice system or legal profession, has its own *language*. Terms are used to create distinct meanings which satisfy specific objectives for a limited jurisdiction. Like any tool, language is subject to abuse and confusion.

The Pre-Test was offered to validate the significance of language. After years of public e*ducation*, reading, and listening, after being conditioned by government disinformation, many of us may not know the answers to these basic questions.

a)   The *United States* is not the 50 States of the Union.

b)   An American who lives within the several States may never step within the United States.

c)   Americans may never step within the United States while being deemed as within the United States.

d)   Americans may step within the United States and not be within its jurisdiction.

e)   The foregoing statements are true because the *United States* is a legal fiction created by legalese.

The United States is a fiction, a legal entity, created by language in the Federal Constitution. Title 28 USC 3002 defines the *United States* as a "federal corporation." The entity that is the *United States* has a jurisdiction distinguished by territory, property, persons, and power unique to its existence. The *United States* is a place we may never enter unless and until we are within a federal courthouse, post office, a national forest, or any other federal venue. As such, we may not enter the jurisdiction of the United States unless or until we accept a federal benefit or privilege, like Social Security or becoming an *employee* in relation to the government.

The significance of this explanation should be apparent. If we do not understand the language, we will not understand the message, which will undoubtedly affect our individual and collective well-being. This examination should motivate us to become more enlightened as to a language which has profound direct and indirect repercussions.

Consider an illustration. Imagine a caveman creating his own autonomous domain. He establishes "Campsite Ugh" (a fiction like the United States) with legal language (Federal Constitution). He does this by grunting, gesturing, and drawing a crude circle with his wooden club around the circumference of the site (think of Washington DC and federal territory). He grunts and pounds his chest, which are elements of language (legalese), to declare (force of law) that the land, woman, child, fire, and deer carcass (property in his jurisdiction), within the "Campsite Ugh" (United States), are within his power alone. All who hear and see this aggrandizing *Act* know this "governing power" controls what it "legally" possesses. Through the cavemen's authority, the observer recognizes that the caveman is not asserting influence over persons and property without (outside) of his jurisdiction. Now, is this analogy any different than the *United States*?

Before we define legal terms within the federal codes and regulations, consider how terms may be limited or expanded. Legal terms are further narrowed by the concepts of "noscitur a sociis" and "ejusdem generis."

> The maxim noscitur a sociis, that **a word is known by the company it keeps**, while not an inescapable rule, is often wisely applied where a word is capable of many meanings in order **to avoid giving of unintended breadth to the Acts of Congress**. *Jarecki v G.D. Searle & Co.*, *367 US 303, 307 (1961)*

> Sec. 30. Judicial Definitions of income. By the rule of construction, noscitur a sociis, however, **the words in this statute must be construed in connection with those to which it is joined,** namely, gains and profits; and it is evidently **the intention**, as a general rule, to **tax only the profit… not his whole revenue**. *Roger Foster, "A Treatise on the Federal Income Tax Under the Act of 1913", pg 142*

> Under the principle of ejusdem generis, when a general term follows a specific one, the **general term should be understood as** a reference to subjects **akin to the one with specific enumeration**. *Norfolk & Western R. Co., v Train Dispatchers*, *499 US 117, 129 (1991)*

Now consider the following translations and definitions.

Expressio unius personae uel rei est exclusion alterius. The **express mention of one** person or thing in a written instrument **is equivalent to the express exclusion of all other persons or things.**

Inclusio unius est exclusion alterius. The **inclusion of one is the exclusion of another**. The certain designation of one person is an absolute exclusion of all others... This doctrine decrees that where law expressly describes particular situation to which it shall apply, an irrefutable reference must be drawn that **what is omitted or excluded was intended to be omitted or excluded**. *Black's Law Dictionary, 6th Ed.*

As we weigh definitions which contain the terms "includes" and "including," consider the following citations within the federal tax code and regulations.

The terms "includes" and "including" **do not exclude** things enumerated **which are in the same general class.** *26 CFR, Chapter 26, Internal Revenue, Chapter 1 Internal Revenue Service Department of the Treasury, Subchapter F Procedure and Administration. Part 403 Disposition of Seized Property 403.5 Meaning of Terms.*

(c) Includes and including. The term "includes" and "including" when used in a definition contained in this title **shall not be deemed to exclude** other **things otherwise within** the meaning of the word defined. *Title 26 Internal revenue Code, Subtitle F Procedure and Administration, Chapter 79, Section 7701(c) Definitions.*

Does the tax code cover (include) anything and everything based upon the foregoing definitions? Notice what may not be excluded: things "in the same general class" and "things otherwise within the meaning of the word defined." The definition of *includes* and *including* is limited even within the tax code. This point is confirmed when we view the following:

> Sec. 61(a) GENERAL DEFINITION. – Except as otherwise provided, gross income means all income from whatever source derived, including (but not limited to) the following items...

The phrase "but not limited to" allows the government to include those items which may be added in the future and are otherwise only "income from whatever source derived."

The Supreme Court determined that the Utah Supreme Court incorrectly enlarged the meaning of the term "including."

> The Court also considered that the word "including" was used as a word of enlargement, the learned court being of the opinion that such was its ordinary sense. With this we cannot concur. *Montello Salt Co., v Utah*, 221 US 452 (1911)

> It is axiomatic that **the statutory definition of the term excludes** unstated meanings of that term. *Meese v Keene*, 481 US 465, 466 (1987)

> [W]here Congress includes particular language in one section of a statute but omits it in another section of the same Act, **it is generally presumed that Congress acts** intentionally and **purposely in the disparate inclusion or exclusion**. *Russello v United States*, 464 US 16, 23 (1983)

With the definitions of the terms *includes and including*, let's make a simple comparison of two separate sections within the tax code which define the term *United States*.

4612. Definitions and special rules

(a) Definitions. For purposes of this subchapter

(4) United States.

In general. The term "United States" means the 50 States, the District of Columbia, the Commonwealth of Puerto Rico, any possession of the United States, the Commonwealth of the Northern Mariana Islands, and the Trust Territory of the Pacific Islands. *Section 4612, Subtitle D, Chapter 38, Subchapter C General Provisions.*

3121 (e)(2) United States

The term "United States" when used in a geographical sense **includes** the Commonwealth of **Puerto Rico, the Virgin Islands, Guam, and American Samoa**. *26 CFR, Subtitle C Employment taxes and collection of income tax, Chapter 21 Federal Insurance Contributions Act, Subchapter C General Provisions.*

The *United States* is not and cannot be the same in each example. Section 4612 deals with an excise tax on oil, a legitimate exaction within the 50 States, while section 3121 deals with an excise tax for FICA—Social Security and Medicaid. Each definition satisfies an intended purpose, which is why they are dissimilar. The term *includes* serves the purpose of limiting. Ask whether or not the *United States* in section 3121 is limited to the territories listed. Keep in mind, we want to understand how the United States (Government) acquires or presumes jurisdiction over Americans for income tax purposes. Knowing how and why terms are used is critical. It would stand to reason that any of the 50 States may choose to enter the *United States* to participate in a federal program. But any failure to do so would leave that State *without the jurisdiction of the United States* for that purpose.

Let's define the term "State" under section 3121.

(1) The term "state" **includes the District of Columbia, the Commonwealth of Puerto Rico, the Virgin Islands, Guam and American Samoa.** *26 USC 3121*

In light of noscis a sociis and ejusdem generis, compare the definition in 3121 with the following:

3371. Definitions.

(1) "State" means

(A) **a state of the United States, the District of Columbia, the Commonwealth of Puerto Rico**, the **Trust Territory of the Pacific Islands, and a territory or possession of the United States**; and

(B) **an instrumentality or authority of a State or States as defined in subparagraph (A)** of this paragraph (1) and a Federal-State authority or instrumentality. Subchapter VI. Assignments to and from States. *Chapter 33 Examination, Selection and Placement, Subpart B Employment and Retention, Part III Employees, 5 USC Government Organization and Employees*

In both definitions, the District of Columbia is a "State." Also, note section 3371 of Title 5 deals with the "United States Government" and its "employees." The term "State" would obviously be limited to the list provided and exclude those not within this class. It would not include the several States, unless they consented.

Now weigh the significance of the following definition of *State* as defined within the codes of a number of the 50 States.

> (13) "In this state" or "in the state" means within the exterior limits of the Commonwealth and **includes all territory within these limits owned by or ceded to the United States of America.**[19]

Whatever property was conveyed to the *United States* is defined for the purposes of a given code section as being within the *State*. Meanwhile, it is common knowledge that territory belonging to the United States Government is exclusive to it alone. What could be the purpose of this contrary definition? Equally notable, this definition is congruent with that of *State* within 4 USC 110(d) and 110(e), known as The Buck Act (4 USC 104-113).

> **110(d)** The term "State" includes any Territory or possession of the United States.
> **110(e)** The term "Federal area" means any lands or premises held or acquired by or for the use of the United States or any department, establishment, or agency, of the United States; and any Federal area, or any part thereof, which is located within the exterior boundaries of any State, shall be deemed to be a Federal area located within such State.

The 1940 Buck Act allows for the creation of a "Federal area" for application and enforcement of the Public Salary Tax Act of 1939 under section 111, while the balance of its enforcement falls under the tax code. Note the defined purpose of this Act.

> (a)GENERAL RULE.—
> The United States **consents to the taxation of pay or compensation for personal service** as an **officer or employee of the United States**, a territory or possession or political subdivision thereof, the government of the District

---

[19] http://www.lrc.ky.gov/statutes/statute.aspx?id=39929

of Columbia, or an agency **or instrumentality** of one or more of the foregoing, **by a duly constituted taxing authority having jurisdiction**, if the taxation does not discriminate against the officer or employee because of the source of the pay or compensation. *4 USC 111*

Is there any surprise the majority of the 50 States have a *State* income tax which corresponds with the submission of federal tax returns by *employees within the United States*? Are States merely taxing *federal employees* within a "Federal area" within the "exterior boundaries of any State?" The Buck Act establishes the authority for the States to collect income and sales taxes within a Federal area—land owned or controlled by any agency or branch of the government—within its borders.

Based upon legal terms, is it reasonable to conclude a man is within *the United States* and the *State* of the District of Columbia or any other *State* of the *United States* when he voluntarily agrees to enter the "relation of employment" and receives the federal benefit of Social Security or files a federal income tax return? Do these decisions or actions grant a federal status and liability for the income tax? Answer this query by reviewing the definition of *United States* by the Supreme Court.

> (1) It may be the name of a sovereign nation occupying the position of other sovereigns in the family of nations. (2) It may designate the limited territory, the ten square mile area… in the Constitution, over which the sovereignty of the federal government extends. (3) It may be the collective name of the 50 States which are united by and under the Constitution as the "united States of America." Hooven & Allison Co. v. Evatt, 324 US 652(1945)

Compare this definition with *United States* and *State* within the tax code.

> (9) United States

The term "United States" when used in a geographical sense **includes only the States and the District of Columbia.** *26 USC 7701*

(10) State
The term "State" shall be construed to **include the District of Columbia**, where such construction is necessary to carry out the provisions of this title. *26 USC 7701*

Note the difference between these definitions compared to sections 3121, 3371, and 4612. The use of *includes* is limiting. Consider yet another definition of *State* within section 6103(b)(5) of the tax code, which concerns "Procedure and Administration," which is distinct from enforcement.

(B) DEFINITIONS. - For purposes of this section-
(5) STATE. - The term "State" means - any of the 50 States, the District of Columbia, the Commonwealth of Puerto Rico, the Virgin Islands, the Canal Zone, Guam, American Samoa, and the Commonwealth of the Northern Mariana Islands, and...

Consider the definition for "United States person."

(30) United States person.
The term "United States person" means –
(A) a **citizen or resident** of the **United States**
(B) a domestic partnership
(C) a domestic corporation
(D) any estate (other than a foreign estate within the meaning of paragraph (31)), and
(E) any trust if
(i) a court **within the United States** is able to exercise primary supervision over the administration of the trust, and

(ii) one or more **United States persons** have the authority to control all substantial decisions of the trust. 26 USC 7701

Notice the foregoing comprises a list of a class for what is a *United States person*. Recall that a legal definition exists solely to satisfy the custom purpose of the term and specific code section. Legal terms do not square with a common understanding of the word. Note that each is a creation of or designation by the Federal Government. *United States person* serves a limited purpose—to classify those within the *United States*. Are those who voluntarily accept Social Security and employment and file U. S. Individual Income Tax Returns *U. S. persons*?

Are you a *United States person*? Are *United States citizens* and *residents* any different? Are citizens who subscribe to Social Security or file federal tax returns designated as *U. S. persons* and *United States citizens* once they enter within the jurisdiction of the *United States*?

104 Citizen of the United States.
In this title, the term "**citizen of the United States**," when used in reference to a **natural person, means an individual who is a national** of the United States as **defined in** section **101(a)(22) of the Immigration and Nationality Act**. *46 USC Shipping, Subtitle I General, Chapter 1 Definitions*.

78 dd-1 Prohibited Foreign Exchange Practices by Issuers
(1) As used in this subsection, the term "**United States person" means a national of the United States (as defined in** section 101 of **the Immigration and Nationality Act (8 USC** 1101) or **any corporation, partnership, association, joint stock company, business trust, unincorporated**

organization, or sole proprietorship organized under the laws of the United States or any State, territory, possession or commonwealth of the United States or any political subdivision thereof. *15 USC Commerce and Trade Chapter 2B Securities Exchanges*

141.31 General requirements and definitions.
Definitions of resident or nonresident.
(d)For the purposes of this subpart, "resident" means **an individual who resides within**, or a partnership, or one or more of whose partners reside within **the customs territory of the United States or the Virgin Islands of the United States**, or **a corporation** incorporated in and jurisdiction **within the customs territory of the United States or** in **the Virgin Islands of the United States**. A **"nonresident" means an individual**, partnership or corporation **not meeting the definition of "resident."** *19 CFR Customs Duties, Chapter 1 United States Customs and Border Protection Department of Homeland Security, Department of the Treasury, Part 141 – Entry of Merchandise, Subpart C – Powers of Attorney*

As defined, are you a *United States citizen*, a *United States person,* or a *resident*? Note, a *citizen of the United States*, (Section 104) is limited to immigrants within the regulations for "Shipping." The definition specifically references 8 USC which deals with "Immigration and Nationality." The term cannot apply to anyone other than the designated class. The same is true for the definition of *United States person* under 15 USC. However, in addition to immigrants, the list includes fictions created, classified, or designated as such by the federal government. The list does not include Citizens of the several States.

The term "resident" under 19 CFR is within the "customs territory" of the *United States*. Note, the IRS is authorized to enforce the income tax within the Internal Revenue Districts according to 26 USC 7601. The President of the United States is, according to 26 USC 7621, authorized to define the internal revenue districts. The President delegated the Secretary of the Treasury, via Executive Order 10289 in 1952, which is still in effect, to designate these districts. The Secretary of the Treasury defined the internal revenue districts in Treasury Order 150-01. Currently, Treasury Order 150-02, which superseded 150-01, was signed in 1998, coinciding with the IRS Restructuring and Reform Act of 1998. Significantly, this new order established the offices (as in public offices) essential to administer the tax code in the District of Columbia. Is there one internal revenue district and is it Washington, D.C–the *United States*?

Those who are within the class of *U.S. persons* fill a "public office" and deemed "residents" within the "customs territory of the *United States* or its *States*. Why is there any reason to define the term *United States person*, unless there is a unique definition that is not and cannot be applied at everyone?

Consider the following quotes as confirmation there is a distinction between an *American* and a *United States citizen*:

> A "U.S. Citizen" upon leaving the District of Columbia becomes involved in "interstate commerce", as a "resident" does not have the common-law right to travel, of a Citizen of one of the several States. Hendrick v Maryland S.C. Reporter's Rd. 610-625 (1914)

Are all people who secure a "Drivers License" *U.S. Citizens*?

> ...the privileges and immunities of **citizens of the United States** do not necessarily include all the rights protected by

the first eight amendments to the Federal Constitution against the powers of the Federal Government. Maxwell v Dow, 20 SCR 448 at 455

United States citizens do not receive protection against the *United States* Government inherent with constitutional constraints of the first eight amendments.

The only absolute and unqualified right of a **United States citizen is to residence within the territorial boundaries of the United States**... U.S. v Valentine, 288 F. Supp. 957

Therefore, the **U.S. citizens** *residing in one of the states of the union, are classified as property and franchises of the federal government as an* **"individual entity."** Wheeling Steel Corp v Fox, 298 U.S. 193 (1936)

The rights and privileges, and immunities which the fourteenth constitutional amendment and Rev. St. section 1979, for its enforcement, were designated to protect, are such as belonging to citizens of the United States as such, and not as citizens of a state". Wadleigh v. Newhall 136 F. 941 (1905)6

We have in our political system a Government of the United States and a government of each of the several states. Each is distinct from the other and each has citizens of its own...U.S. v. Cruikshank, 92 U.S. 542 (1876)

In the Constitution of the United States **the word "citizen"** is generally, if not always, used in a political sense **to designate one who has the rights and privileges of a citizen of a state or of the United States**. It is also used in the first section of the Fourteenth Amendment. *Baldwin v. Franks, 120 U.S. 678*

A person is born subject to the jurisdiction of the United States, for purposes of acquiring citizenship at birth, if his or her birth occurs in **territory** over which the United States is sovereign, even though another country provides all governmental services within the territory, and the territory is subsequently ceded to the other country. *3C Am Jur 2d, Aliens and Citizens, §2689, Who is born in United States and subject to United States jurisdiction*

Citizenship of the United States is defined by the Fourteenth Amendment and federal statutes, but the requirements for **citizenship of a state generally depend not upon definition but the constitutional or statutory context** in which the term is used. Risewick v. Davis, 19 Md. 82, 93 (1862); Halaby v. Board of Directors of University of Cincinnati, 162 Ohio St. 290, 293, 123 N.E.2d 3 (1954) and authorities therein cited.

...he was not a citizen of the United States, he was a citizen and voter of the State, ... One may be a citizen of a State and yet not a citizen of the United States. McDonel v. The State, 90 Ind. 320 (1883)]

Referring back to the definitions of terms within the tax code, who is a *U.S. person*? Are those who willingly subscribe to Social Security and enter the "relation of employment" or file federal income tax returns *U.S. persons* within the jurisdiction of the *State* which comprises the *United States* for the purpose of the income tax and application of the tax code? It does not matter that the term *State* or *United States* does not include the several States, the 50 States. As employees and recipients of a federal benefit, or with the designation of a federal status associated with the filing of tax forms, the limited scope of these terms is legally sufficient. These are the only definitions required, as no others would be appropriate.

Let's follow this reasoning. The *United States* may not tax the labor or earnings of Americans unless by Apportionment. If Americans knowingly or unknowingly change their status or class, they become *U.S. persons*. They may live within the several States, but their *income* (wages) is excised for the federal privileges and status they enjoy–*within the jurisdiction of the United States*, within the scope of the tax code.

Are you a *United States person*? Under the concept of noscitur a sociis and ejusdem generis, within the tax code, the definition of *United States person* is a listing of government creations or fictions or a means of identification. Thus, *U.S. person* is a title, status, classification, or designation with a legal purpose. Are *United States citizens* and *residents* any different? Or are *U.S. citizens* who subscribe to Social Security or file federal tax returns designated as *U.S. persons* once they enter into the jurisdiction of the *United States*?

Note the following definitions within the tax code which will enable us to comprehend the statues and regulations.

Trade or Business
The term "trade or business" **includes the performance of the functions of a public office.** *26 USC, Subtitle F Procedures and Administration, Chapter 79 Definitions.*

26 USC 3401 – Definitions.
(c) For purposes of this chapter, the term **"employee" includes an officer, employee, or elected official of the United States, a State or any political subdivision thereof, or instrumentality of any one or more of the foregoing.** The term "employee" also includes an officer of a corporation.

Puerto Rico, Virgin Islands, Guam, American Samoa Employers
District of Columbia   employees   Residents   federal
forms - W-2, W-4, 1099 United States citizen   1040 forms

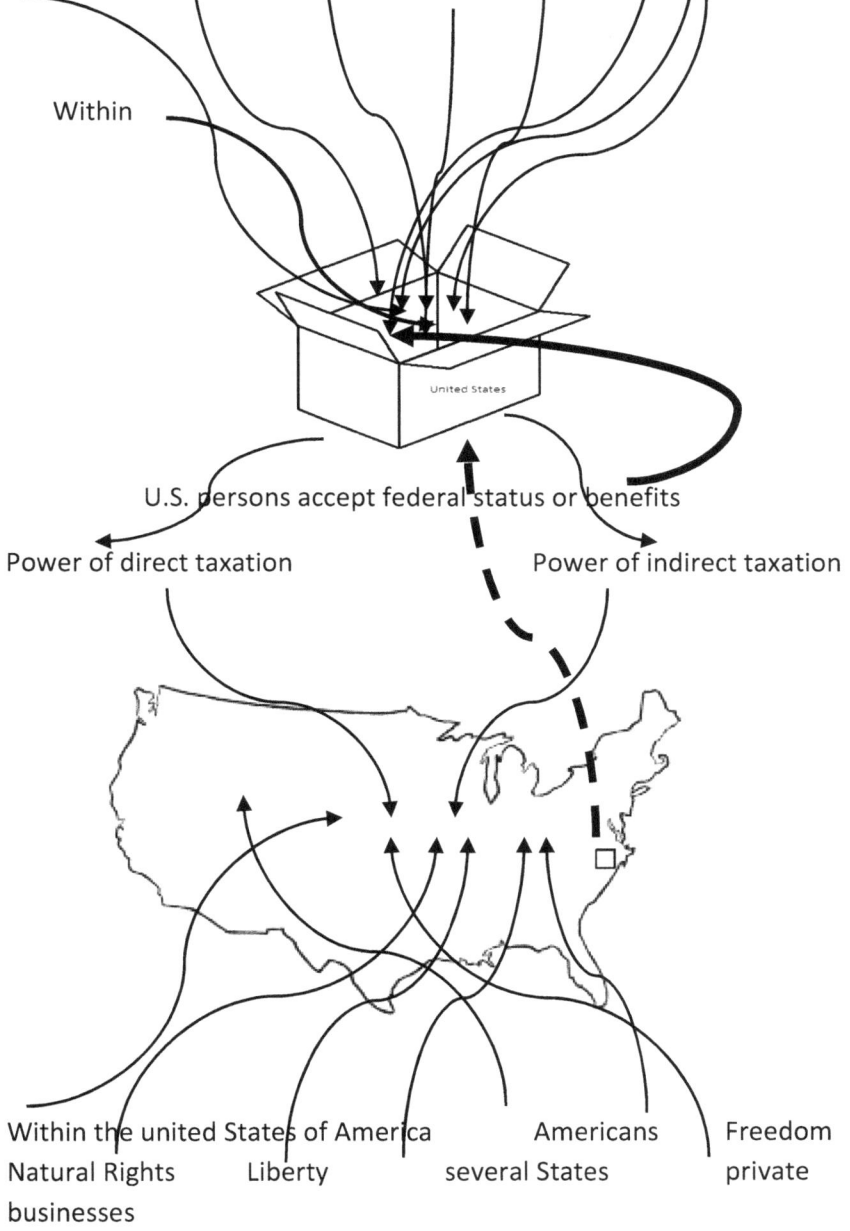

Within

United States

U.S. persons accept federal status or benefits

Power of direct taxation   Power of indirect taxation

Within the united States of America   Americans   Freedom
Natural Rights   Liberty   several States   private
businesses

Becoming a Taxpayer

This is America.

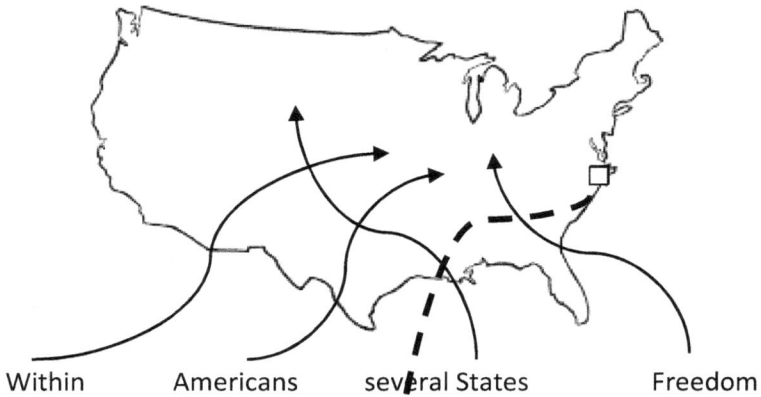

| Within | Americans | several States | Freedom |

Americans are born within America–a land of freedom and unalienable rights and comprised of the several States, the 50 States of the Union, the united States of America.

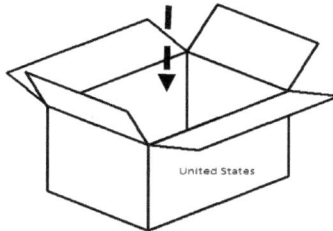

United States

When Americans accept a federal status or benefit, they effectively leave the realm of freedom and enter within the United States. **Note: the Constitution does not apply within the *United States*.**

Americans are within the United States once they accept a federal federal privilege or benefit

The District of Columbia, Guam, Puerto Rico, the Virgin Islands, federal territories, possessions

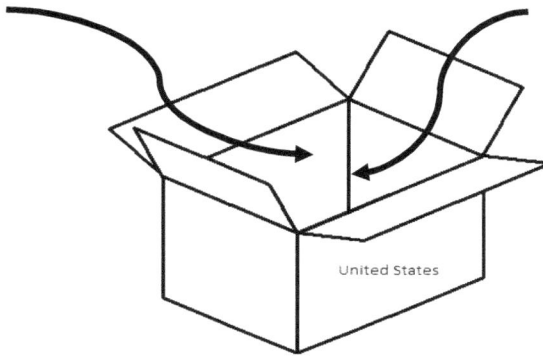

United States

Tax Return

United States

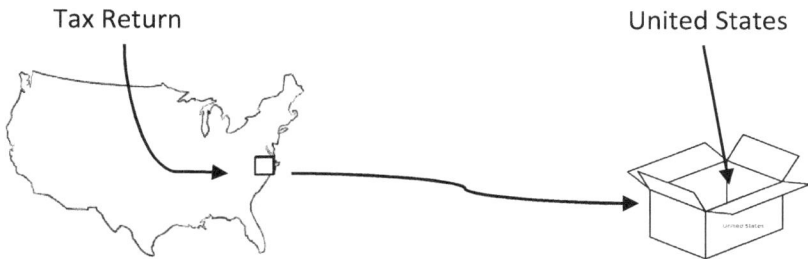

When Americans file federal tax forms and accept a classification which places them within the jurisdiction of the *United States*, the Government recognizes them as *employees*.

Taxpayers

Washington D.C.

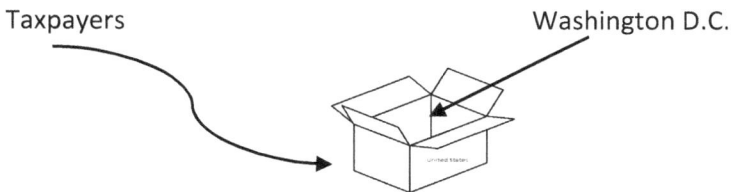

For income tax purposes, the *United States* does not view Americans with a natural right to labor (property) and earnings, (property), but as "U.S. Persons," "individuals," and "taxpayers" subject to excise upon "wages."

Early American History

1)   In 1776, the world witnessed the birth of a country that acknowledged the inherent natural rights of the people. As long as one did not violate another's life, liberty, or property, he could work, contract, associate, worship, speak, love, laugh, cry, strive, thrive, live, and die in freedom.

2)   The people formed "free and independent States" with governments of limited powers and jurisdiction, constrained by written constitutions. All powers not granted to the States were retained by the people.

> The States between each other are sovereign and independent. They are distinct and separate sovereignties, except so far as they have parted with some of the attributes of sovereignty by the Constitution. They continue to be nations, with all their rights, and under all their national obligations, and with all the rights of nations in every particular; except in the surrender by each to the common purposes and objects of the Union, under the Constitution. The rights of each State, when not yielded up, remain absolute. *Bank of Augusta v Earle, 38 US 519 (1839)*

3)   The several States formed a Federal Government known as the *United States* and granted it limited powers in the Constitution under Article 1, Section 8.

> The government of the United States has been emphatically termed a government of laws, and not of men. It will certainly cease to deserve that high appellation, if the laws

furnish no remedy for the violation of a vested right. *Marbury v Madison*, 5 US 137 (1803)

… The governments are but trustees acting under derived authority and have no power to delegate what is not delegated to them. But the people, as the fountain might take away what they have delegated and intrust to whom they please… The sovereignty in every state resides in the people of the state and they may alter and change their form of government at their own pleasure. *Luther v Borden*, 48 US 1 (1841)

4) The Tenth Amendment to the Federal Constitution clarified that powers not delegated to the *United States* were reserved to the States or to the people. The Federal Government was truly limited. The federal and state governments served the people— the sovereigns—as defined by the Supreme Court, for the people were the source of power. Without the people, these governments would not have been formed.

While all sovereign powers are delegated to… the government, sovereignty itself remains with the people… *Yick Wo v. Hopkins*, 118 US 356 (1886)

There is no such thing as a power of inherent sovereignty in the government of the United States… In this country sovereignty resides in the people, and Congress can exercise no power which they have not, by their Constitution entrusted to it: All else is withheld. *Julliard v Greenman*, 110 US 421 (1884)

In determining the boundaries of apparently conflicting powers between states and the general government, the proper question is, not so much what has been, in terms, reserved to the states, as what has been, expressly or by necessary implication, granted by the people to the national government; for each state possesses all the powers of an independent and sovereign nation, except as far as they have been ceded away by the constitution. The federal government is but a creature of the people of the states, and, like an agent appointed for definite and specific purposes, must show an express or necessarily implied authority in the charter of its appointment, to give validity to its acts. *People ex re. Atty. Gen. V. Naglee, 1 Cal 234 (1850)*

The makers of our Constitution undertook to secure conditions favorable to the pursuit of happiness. They recognized the significance of man's spiritual nature, of his feelings and his intellect. They knew that only a part of the pain, pleasure and satisfactions of life are to be found in material things. They sought to protect Americans in their beliefs, their thoughts, their emotions and their sensations. They conferred, as against the Government, the right to be let alone – the most comprehensive of rights and the right most valued by civilized men. *Olmstead v States, 227 US 438, 478 (1928) (Brandeis, J., dissenting) see also Washington v Harper, 494 US 210 (1990)*

5)   The people flourished under this form of government.

Everyman has a natural right to the fruits of his own labor, is generally admitted; and no other person can rightfully deprive him of those fruits, and appropriate them against his will... *The Antelope, 23 US 66 (1825)*

In the general course of human nature, a power over a man's subsistence amounts to a power over his will. *Alexander Hamilton, Federalist Paper No. 79*

6) The Supreme Court stated,

This distinction is essential to the idea of constitutional government. To deny it or blot it obliterates the line of demarcation that separates constitutional government from absolutism, free self-government based on the sovereignty of the people from that despotism, whether of the one or the many, which enables the agent of the state to declare and decree that he is the state; to say, "L'Etat, c'est moi." Of what avail are written constitutions, whose bills of right, for the security of individual liberty, have been written too often with the blood of martyrs shed upon the battle-field and the scaffold, if their limitations and restraints upon power may be overpassed with impunity by the very agencies created and appointed to guard, define, and enforce them; and that, too, with the sacred authority of law, not only compelling obedience, but entitled to respect? And how else can these principles of individual liberty and right be maintained, if, when violated, the judicial tribunals are forbidden to visit penalties upon individual offenders, who are the instruments of wrong, whenever they interpose the shield of the state? The doctrine is not to be tolerated. The whole frame and scheme of the political institutions of this country, state and federal, protest against it. Their continued existence is not compatible with it. It is the doctrine of absolutism, pure, simple and naked, and of communism which is its twin, the double progeny of the same evil birth. *Poindexter v Greenhow, 114 US 270 (1885)*

Men are endowed by their Creator with certain unalienable rights, - "life, liberty, and the pursuit of happiness;" and to "secure" not grant or create, these rights, governments are instituted. That property which a man has honestly acquired he retains full control of, subject to these limitations: First, that he shall not use it to his neighbor's injury, and that does not mean that he must use it for his neighbor's benefit; second, that if he devotes it to a public use, he gives the public a right to control that use; and third, that whenever the public needs require, the public may take it upon payment of due compensation. *Budd v People of State of New York, 143 US 517 (1892)*

7)   With the passage of time, Americans became comfortable and satisfied. Their progress and success and subsequent indifference insulated them from each other and matters of substance. The people became less informed and less engaged in civics and issues of governance.

8)   Confusion increased. Clear distinctions between power and inherent natural rights became blurred. The people no longer knew what was once known and generally accepted. They became accountable to laws and regulations of which they were largely unaware.

9) The ignorance and apathy of the people increased, as did their fear of government. They either failed to assert or lost their rights.

10) By illustration, the people once kept all of their earnings. By natural right, labor and earnings were and are considered "property." Yet, today, people pay a portion of their earnings (wages) to the federal government. What happened? To understand, we must look to history and the Constitution.

11) For hundreds of years, the people knew Congress could not tax their livelihood or property. They knew Congress had but two forms of taxation: direct and indirect.

12) If the government needed to raise money, it could do so only by the rule of apportionment, which meant a State paid a proportional share of the government's request equal to the State's share of the national population. For example, with 10% of the country's population, Virginia would pay 10% of $100 billion. This is the extent of a federal direct tax.

13) The Founding Fathers knew that, historically, governments control and destroy by means of direct taxation. These discerning men believed the Rule of Apportionment would prevent the government from gaining autonomy.

> Thus, Congress having power to regulate commerce with foreign nations, and among the several States, and with the Indian tribes, may, without a doubt, provide for coasting licenses, licenses to pilots, license to trade with the Indians, and any other licenses necessary or proper for the exercise of that great and extensive power; and the same

observation is applicable to every power of Congress, to the exercise of which the granting of licenses may be incident. All such licenses confer authority, and give rights to the licensee. But very different considerations apply to the internal commerce or domestic trade of the States. Over this commerce and trade **Congress has no power of regulation nor any direct control. This power belongs exclusively to the States. No interference by Congress with the business of citizens transacted within a state is warranted by the Constitution, except as such as is strictly incidental to the exercise of powers clearly granted to the legislature.** The power to authorize a business within a State is plainly repugnant to the exclusive power of the State over the same subject. It is true that the power of Congress to tax is a very extensive power. It is given in the Constitution, with only one exception and only two qualifications. Congress cannot tax exports, and it must impose direct taxes by the rule of apportionment, and indirect taxes by the rule of uniformity. Thus limited, and thus only, it reaches every subject, and may be exercised at discretion. **But, it reaches only existing subjects. Congress cannot authorize a trade or business within a State in order to tax it.** *License Tax Cases*, *72 US 462 (1866)*

14) Even today, direct taxation is a viable means of raising revenue for funding the operation of the federal government. Yet, it is a means of taxation that is no longer used.

15) Indirect taxes are duties, imposts, and excises. According to the Supreme Court,

Excises are "taxes laid upon the manufacture, sale or consumption of commodities within the country, upon license to pursue certain occupations, and upon corporate privileges." *Cooley, Const. Lim. 7th ed 680. Flint v Stone Tracy Co., 220 US 107, 151 (1911)*

A lower court stated,

> The terms **"excise tax" and "privilege tax" are synonymous**. The two are often used interchangeably. *American Airways v Wallace, 57 F 2d 877, 880 (MD Tenn. 1932)*

16)   There are two key aspects to an excise tax. First, excises must be uniform across the country. Second, excise taxes are paid on a voluntary basis only when one chooses to participate in an activity or privilege for which an excise is assessed. For example, if a man chooses to buy gasoline, he would pay the excise voluntarily. This is true for other commodities.

17)   In 1862, the federal government enacted a tax upon those who were in the "employment or service of the United States," those who were employees for the federal government. The United States could only tax those who were within the jurisdiction of the *United States*.

> Sec. 86. And be it further enacted, That on and after the first day of August, eighteen hundred sixty-two, **there shall be levied, collected, and paid on all salaries of officers**, or payments to persons in **the civil, military, naval, or other employment or service of the United States,** including senators and representatives and delegates in Congress, when exceeding the rate of six hundred dollars per annum, a

duty of three per centum on the excess above the said six hundred dollars; and it shall be the duty of all paymasters, and all disbursing officers, under the government of the United States, or in the employ thereof, when making any payments to officers and persons as aforesaid, or upon settling and adjusting the accounts of such officers and persons, to deduct and withhold the aforesaid duty of three per centum, and shall, at the same time, make a stating the name of the officer or person from whom such deduction was made, and the amount thereof, which shall be transmitted to the office of the Commissioner of Internal revenue, and entered as part of the internal duties...

18) Americans, who did not work for the federal government, knew they were not required to pay this income tax. They were not exercising a *privilege*. Americans knew the tax was an excise upon those who chose to work for the government, those who made a voluntary decision to accept such *employment*. It is not a natural right to work for the government. Rather, it is a privilege subject to federal excise.

The United States Government receives it limited powers under Article 1, Section 8 of the Constitution. Those powers not granted to the United States are reserved by the States per the 10th Amendment.

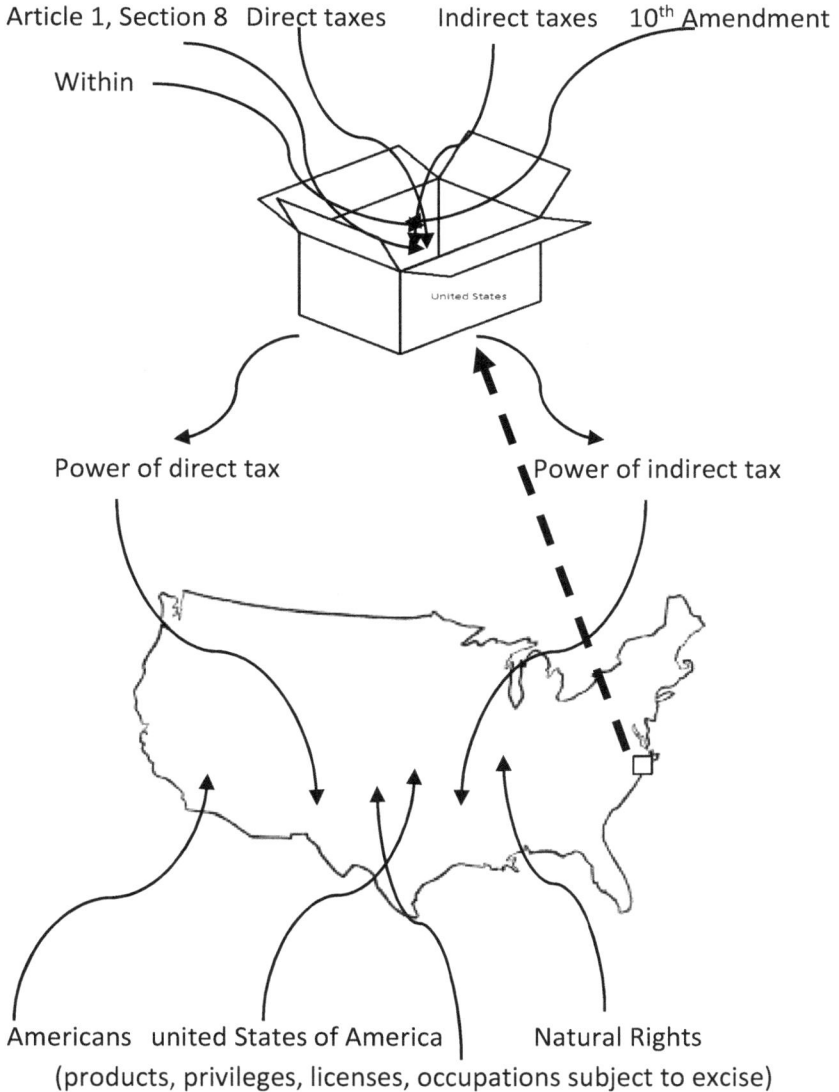

Article 1, Section 8   Direct taxes   Indirect taxes   10th Amendment

Within

United States

Power of direct tax   Power of indirect tax

Americans   united States of America   Natural Rights
(products, privileges, licenses, occupations subject to excise)

Supreme Court Decides, Congress Responds

19)   The Court rendered a decision which further validated that a man's property could be taxed only by Rule of Apportionment.

20)   In 1894, after an income tax act was passed, a man by the name of Pollock filed a lawsuit when his rental income from real estate was taxed. Pollock argued the property could not be taxed directly. Note, Pollock's earnings from his labor were not the subject of the suit. In 1895, Americans knew a man's personal earnings could not be taxed unless by apportionment.

21)   The Supreme Court agreed with Pollock. Yet, the Court made a serious mistake according to Congress. Congressional intent was not to tax property directly, a violation of the Constitution, but to tax the *income* derived from the investment.

22)   As a result of the Pollock decision, Congress had to clarify that the property was not the subject of the tax. To rectify this situation, Congress wrote the Sixteenth Amendment.

> Congress shall have power to lay and collect taxes on **incomes**, from whatever **source derived**, without apportionment among the several States, and without regard to census or enumeration. *Sixteenth Amendment, ratified in 1913*

23)   The Supreme Court specifically defined the term *income*.

> ... there would seem to be no room to doubt that the word [income] must be given the same meaning in all of the Income Tax Act, and that what that meaning is has now

become definitely settled by decisions of this Court. *Merchants' Loan & Trust Co., v Smietanka, 255 US 509 (1921)* [brackets added]

In determining the definition of the word **"income"** thus arrived at, this court has consistently refused to enter into the refinements of lexicographers or economists, and has approved, in the definitions quoted, what **is believed to be the** commonly understood **meaning** of the term which must have been **in the minds of the people when they adopted the 16th Amendment** to the Constitution. *Id. page 519*

The Court further stated,

… it is palpable that it was a "gain" or "profit" "produced by," or "derived from," that investment, and that it "proceeded," and was "severed," or rendered severable, from it, by the sale for cash, and thereby became the "realized gain" which has been repeatedly declared to be taxable income within the meaning of the constitutional amendment and the acts of Congress. (quoting <u>Doyle v Mitchell Bros. Co</u>. and <u>Eisner v Macomber</u>) *Id*.

Consider that,

There must be a gain before there is 'income' within the 16th Amendment. *26 USCA Const. Am 16*

24)   The 16th Amendment clarified congressional intent that income, and not property, is the *source* subjected to the excise tax. Income, *from whatever source derived,* is taxable, but not by the Rule of Apportionment (direct taxation).

... the amendment made it possible to **bring investment income within the scope** of the general income tax law, but did not change the character of the tax. It is still fundamentally **an excise tax or duty with respect to the privilege of   carrying on any activity or owning any property which produces income.** *F. Morse Hubbard, Treasury Department, Legislative Draftsman, House Congressional Record, March 27, 1943, pg. 2580*

The income tax... is an excise tax with respect to **certain activities and privileges** which is measured by reference to the income which they produce. The income is not the subject of the tax; it is the basis for determining the amount of the tax. *Id.*

25) The term "privilege" is defined as:

PRIVILEGE. A particular **benefit or advantage enjoyed by a person, company, or class** beyond the common advantages of other citizens. An exceptional or extraordinary power of exemption. A particular right, advantage, exemption, power, franchise, or immunity held by a person or class, not generally possessed by others. *Black's Law Dictionary, 6th Edition.*

26) The common man does not work by *privilege*. Man is not within a distinct class. He works as a matter of natural right. He has to work to survive. Man does not receive *income*. He merely exchanges his property—his labor—for another form of property, which he uses to survive and thrive.

27) *Income* is not *derived* from man's labor. The Supreme Court addressed the severability of income and how it is derived.

> The government, although basing its argument upon the definition as quoted, placed chief **emphasis upon the word "gain,"** which was extended to include a variety of meanings; while the significance of the next three words was either overlooked or misconceived, - **"derived-from-capital,"** – "the gain-derived-from-capital" etc. Here we have the essential matter: not a gain accruing to capital, not a growth of increment of value in the investment; but a gain, a profit, something of exchangeable value proceeding from the property, severed from the capital, however invested or employed, and coming in, being "derived," that is, received or drawn by the recipient (the taxpayer) for his separate use, benefit and disposal; that is income derived from property. **Nothing else answers the description.** *Eisner v Macomber, 2523 US 189, 207 (1920)*

28) In 1913, Congress passed a new income tax act. Congress was confident the 16th Amendment resolved the confusion concerning income (profit).

29) However, a man named Brushaber filed suit when his investments were taxed. Brushaber's personal earnings were not taxed. In 1913, people knew a man's earnings were property taxable only by apportionment.

30) In Brushaber v Union Pacific R.R. Co., 240 US 1 (1916), the Supreme Court reversed its decision in Pollock v Farmers' & Loan Trust Company, 157 US 429 (1895). The Court ruled the tax was not on property (Brushaber's stocks), but on the income

generated and derived from the stocks. White, who wrote the dissenting opinion in <u>Pollock</u>, was now Chief Justice. He wrote the <u>Brushaber</u> decision.

31)   White articulated that if Congress ever taxed in a manner that was direct in nature, "substance" would supersede "form" and the Rule of Apportionment would apply.

> Moreover, in addition, the conclusion reached in the Pollock Case did not in any degree involve holding that income taxes generically and necessarily came within this class of direct taxes on property, but, on the contrary, recognized the fact that taxation on **income was in its nature an excise entitled to be enforced as such unless and until it was concluded that to enforce it would amount to accomplishing the result which the requirement as to the apportionment of direct taxation was adopted to prevent**, in which case the duty would arise to disregard form and consider substance alone, and hence subject the tax to the regulation as to apportionment which would not otherwise apply to it. <u>*Brushaber v Union Pacific R.R. CO.,*</u> *240 US 1, 17 (1916)*

32)   The 16th Amendment did not provide Congress with the latitude to tax anything and everything.

> I assume that every lawyer will agree with me that we **can not legislatively interpret** the **meaning of the word "income."** That is purely a judicial matter... The word income has a **well defined** meaning **before the amendment** of the constitution was adopted. It has been defined in all of the courts of this country as gains and profits... **If we could call anything that we pleased income, we could obliterate**

all the distinction between income and principal. The Congress cannot affect the meaning of the word "income" by any legislation whatever… Obviously, the people of this country did not intend to give Congress the power to levy a direct tax upon all property of this country without apportionment. *Senator Albert Cummins, 1913 Congressional Record, pg 3843, 3844*

33)   To understand how a man's *earnings* supposedly became taxable, we must explore history. For we now know that a man's livelihood was not a *taxable source of income* under the 16th Amendment. From the passage of the 16th Amendment until the passage of the Social Security Act in 1935, only a small percentage of Americans paid an income tax. Why? Only the wealthy received *income from sources* from which *profit and gain* were derived.

> For 1936, taxable income returns filed represented only 3.9% of the population. *"Collection at Source of the Individual Normal Income Tax", Treasury Department Division of Tax Research, 1941*

> The largest portion of consumer incomes in the United States is not subject to income taxation. Likewise, only a small proportion of the population of the United States is covered by the income tax.

Why was there only a small percentage paying the income tax? The answer is that *income* was realized from profit and gain. A man's earnings were not a source of income.

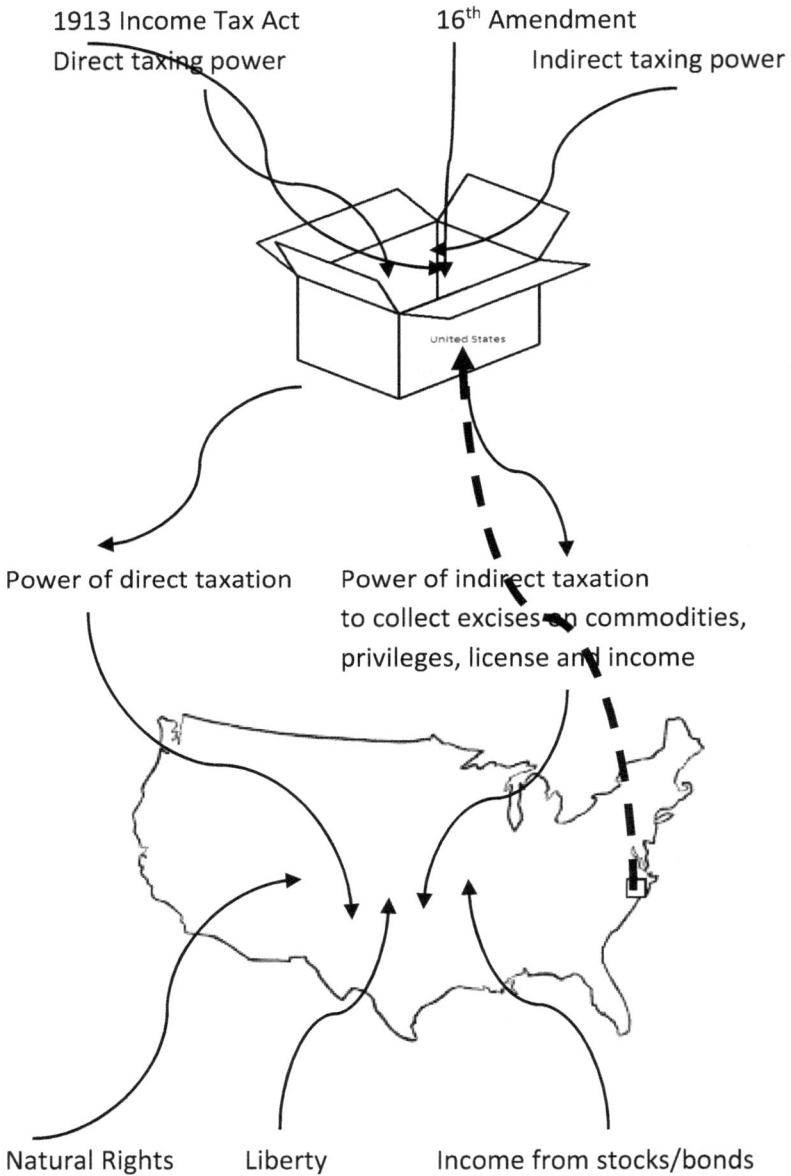

1913 Income Tax Act
Direct taxing power

16th Amendment
Indirect taxing power

United States

Power of direct taxation

Power of indirect taxation to collect excises on commodities, privileges, license and income

Natural Rights   Liberty   Income from stocks/bonds

Social Security and Socialism

34)   In the aftermath of the 1929 stock market crash and the Depression, America experienced grave financial hardships. Congress passed legislation in an attempt to ameliorate the pain and suffering. The people, regrettably, became more dependent upon the federal government.

35)   In 1935, Congress passed the Social Security Act. This scheme was to help in a number of ways including, but not limited to, old age and unemployment benefits. This program was offered to the 50 States and could easily terminate their participation.

36)   When the States subscribed to the federal social insurance scheme, sovereign State Citizens were *not* required to participate or obtain a Social Security number. The following text indicates that not everyone may be assigned a number.

> Title 20 – Employees' Benefits, Chapter III – Social Security Administration, Part 422 – organization and Procedures – Table of Contents, Subpart B – General Procedures, Sec. 422.104 Who can be assigned a social security number.
>
> (a) persons eligible for SSN assignment. We can assign you a social security number **if you meet the evidence requirements** in Sec. 422.107 and you are:
> (1) A **United States citizen**; or
> (2) An **alien lawfully admitted in the United States** (sec. 422.105 describes how we determine if a nonimmigrant alien is permitted to work in the United States)

37)   What happened? Did the Social Security Act change everything?

38)   When people voluntarily chose to accept the federal benefit of Social Security and submit tax forms and returns, their federal status changed. Americans created the nexus and presumption that they were and are liable for the Social Security tax and the federal income tax. They entered a federal class subject to federal excise, not unlike *employees* subject to the Income Tax Act of 1862. Americans who subscribed to Social Security entered within the jurisdiction of the federal government. They became *U.S. citizens and U.S. persons within the United States.*

39)   Notably, participation in this scheme obligated Americans to the income tax on wages and the federal income tax as well.

> **In addition to other taxes**, there shall be levied, collected and paid upon **the income of every individual a tax**. *Social Security Act of 1935, Section 801*

40)   Such Americans became defined by the legal terms "taxpayer," "person," "individual," "United States person," and "employee." The employment tax is an internal revenue tax, an excise paid in a uniform manner by those who voluntarily exchanged their right to labor and earnings for a federal status and privilege. Filing of federal forms classified them with and under a federal status.

41)   Title 42 of the United States Code (USC), Public Welfare and Title 20 of the Code of Federal Regulations (CFR), Employees' Benefits cover Social Security. While it is transparent that one

who subscribes to Social Security does not *work* for the federal government, they are deemed employees all the same. The *United States* oversees the federal program for *Employees' Benefits* for all who file the required forms.

42) In 1937, the Social Security Act was challenged. The Supreme Court established that the Social Security Act as an "income tax on employees" and an "excise tax on employers" for having individuals in their employ.

> The tax, which is described in the statute as an excise, is laid with uniformity throughout the United States as a duty, import or excise upon **the relation of employment**. *Charles C. Steward Machine Company v Davis*, 301 US 548, 578 (1937)

The Supreme Court stated in a separate case that the Social Security Act, under Title VIII,

> Lays two different types of tax, an "**income tax on employees**," and "an excise tax on employers." The **income tax on employees is measured by wages** paid during the calendar year. Section 801. The excise tax on the employer is to be paid "with respect to having individuals in his employ," and, like the tax on employees, is measured by wages. *Helvering v Davis*, 301 US 619, 635, (1937)

43) Later the Supreme Court stated,

> The Social Security system may be accurately described as a **form of social insurance** enacted pursuant to Congress'

power to "**spend money in aid of the 'general welfare,'**" Helvering v Davis, supra, at 640, whereby persons gainfully employed, and those who employ them, are taxed to permit the payment of benefits to the retired and disabled, and their dependents. *Flemming v Nestor, 363 US 603, 610 (1960)*

44)   Did 150 years of limited constitutional taxation change as a result of this social scheme? Did the people know? Did they enter this arrangement with fully informed consent?

45)   We must recall, Americans were liable for the "Victory Tax" around this same time period, a tax for the war which would automatically expire within years of its enactment.

> Prior to World War II, no one outside the government paid income tax; the people were, and understood themselves to be, immune from that tax. During WWII, Congress passed the Victory Tax (56 Stat. 884) to impose an income tax on every individual in the United States of America, something which had not been done by any previous income tax act. Excepted from that tax were those already paying income taxes per I.R.C. 211(a) - nonresident alien individuals with no United States business or office but living in a "contiguous country" and having income from United States sources.

> Because the Victory Tax, a wartime measure, was imposed on individuals in the states of the union (and not countries such as Canada or Mexico), those already taxed by section 211(a) had to be excepted from the Victory Tax or they would be taxed twice. This suggests that the nonresident alien individuals living in "contiguous countries" were in fact

living in states such as Virginia and Maryland - being outside the **United States** (District of Columbia).

The Victory Tax was repealed by <u>section 6 of Income Tax Act of 1944</u>, which in amending the I.R.C. includes the states of the union in the terms "certain foreign countries" (<u>section 6 (b)(3)</u>) and "foreign countries and possessions of the United States" (section 6(b)(4)). This restored the scope of income taxation to what it had been prior to the Victory Tax, as not including individuals in the states of the union.

The states of the union are then seen to be included in the terms "contiguous countries," "certain foreign countries" and "foreign countries and possessions of the United States." This shows that every state of the union is foreign to the United States. Those taxed under I.R.C. 211(a) must then be those living in a state of the union and working for government or one of its agencies - drawing income from "sources within the United States."[20]

46)   The people were adversely affected by the artful use of legal terms and definitions. We know now that legalese is not the same as the common man's way of communicating. Legal terms are used specifically for an intended purpose.

47)   If only for a man's decision to voluntarily accept Social Security or enter the "relation of employment," the federal government no longer considered a man's earnings as his property by natural right. The government taxed *wages* by means of excise for a federal privilege.

---

[20] http://www.constitution.org/tax/us-ic/hist/victorytax.htm

48)   In <u>Steward Machine</u>, the Supreme Court stated,

> **Employment is a business relation, if not itself a business**. It is a relation **without which business could seldom be carried on effectively**. The power to tax the activities and relations that constitute a calling considered as a unit is the power to tax any of them.

49)   The act of *employing* or being *employed* was the focus of the tax. This is no different than the court's effort in <u>Brushaber</u> when it clarified that the tax was not on property (stocks), but on the income (profit) realized.

50)   With and through legislation, Congress uses terms and definitions to achieve specific objectives that would otherwise have been impossible to attain.

51)   This point is demonstrated in <u>Knowlton v Moore</u>. The Supreme Court decided the inheritance tax was not on property, but a tax on the *right* to *transfer* property upon death.

> In other words, the public contribution, which death duties exact, is predicated on the passing of property as the result of death, **as distinct from a tax on property** disassociated from its transmission or receipt by will or the result of intestacy. *Knowlton v Moore*, *178 US 41, 47 (1900)*

52)   The Court distinguished between direct and indirect taxes.

> **Direct taxes bear immediately upon persons**, upon the possession and enjoyment of rights; **indirect taxes are levied upon the happening of an event or exchange**. Id

53)   The income tax on "employment" or the receipt of a federal benefit is constitutional. The tax code is constitutional and deals with the collection of excise taxes, not direct taxes. Both Social Security and the relation of employment are excisable (indirect) in nature. Such is the power of legal terms and concepts.

54)   For the purpose of this particular *income tax*, the federal government views those liable as *employees, United States persons,* and *taxpayers* with a federal status and/or benefits.

55)   Consider one crucial thought. Supreme Court decisions are *settled law*. Until the Court alters its decisions or until Congress changes the existing law, its rulings stand. We must conclude Congress intended to reach this objective.

56)   For years people have argued the income tax was a direct tax on man and his property and, consequently, unconstitutional for lack of apportionment under the direct taxing clause of the Constitution. People argued the 16th Amendment did not grant Congress new taxing powers and a man's earnings were not *income*. They posed a number of arguments which have little to no bearing on the issue. In light of a man's decision to accept Social Security and enter the relation of employment, in light of one's unwitting submission of his first 1040 income tax return, all arguments fail. He is presumed to have a federal status which mandates performance under the tax laws. It is that simple. The income tax code is legitimate. The liability is owed by *U.S. persons* within the jurisdiction of the *United States*.

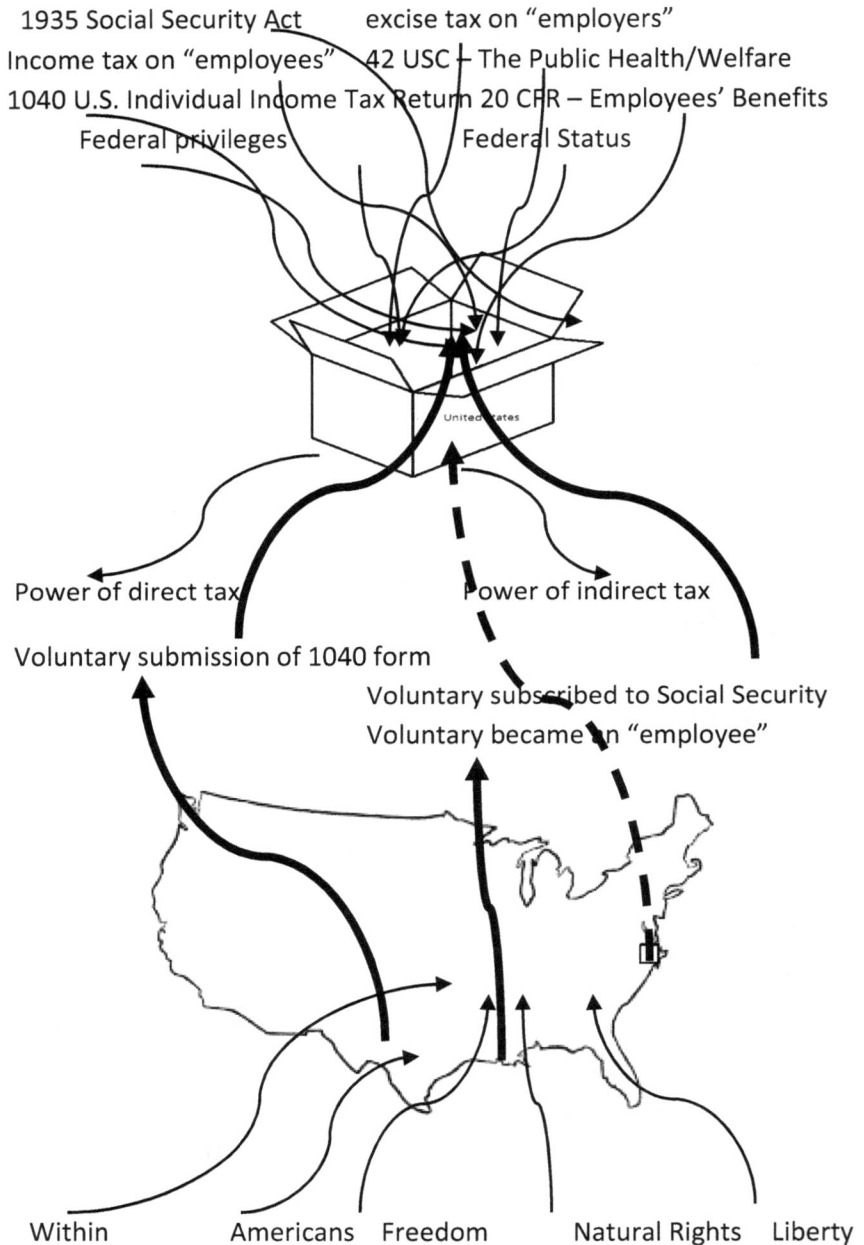

1935 Social Security Act   excise tax on "employers"
Income tax on "employees"   42 USC – The Public Health/Welfare
1040 U.S. Individual Income Tax Return 20 CFR – Employees' Benefits
          Federal privileges   Federal Status

United States

Power of direct tax   Power of indirect tax

Voluntary submission of 1040 form

          Voluntary subscribed to Social Security
          Voluntary became an "employee"

Within   Americans Freedom   Natural Rights   Liberty

Judicial Activism from the Bench

57)   The two Supreme Court cases which solidified the excise tax on wages, <u>Charles C. Steward Machine v Davis</u> and <u>Helvering v Davis</u>, are provided for our understanding. Pay particular attention to the dissenting opinions. These decisions occurred during a turbulent time for America and the Supreme Court. The President's effort to appoint justices who would give credence to this social scheme was a deliberate calculation. There can be no doubt Congress was influenced by the sentiment of the times and prevailing lobbying interests began with the President of the *United States*.

SUPREME COURT OF THE UNITED STATES

No. 837.-OCTOBER TERM, 1936.

Chas. C. Steward Machine Company, Petitioner,

vs.

Harwell G. Davis, Individually and as Collector of Internal Revenue for the District of Alabama, Respondent.

On Writ of Certiorari to the United States Circuit Court of Appeals for the Fifth Circuit.

[May 24, 1937.]

Mr. Justice CARDOZO delivered the opinion of the Court.

The validity of the tax imposed by the Social Security Act on employers of eight or more is here to be determined.

Petitioner, an Alabama corporation, paid a tax in accordance with the statute, filed a claim for refund with the Commissioner of Internal Revenue, and sued to recover the payment ($46.14), asserting a conflict between the statute and the Constitution of the United States. Upon demurrer the District Court gave judgment for the defendant dismissing the complaint, and the Circuit Court of Appeals for the Fifth Circuit affirmed. - F. (2d) -. The decision is in accord with judgments of the Supreme Judicial Court of Massachusetts *(Howes Brothers Co. v. Massachusetts Unemployment Compensation Commission,* December 30, 1936, 5 N. E. (2d) 720), the Supreme Court of California (*Gillum v. Johnson,* November 25, 1936, 62 Pac. (2d) 1037), and the Supreme Court of Alabama *(Beeland Wholesale Co. v. Kaufman,* March 17, 1937, - Ala. -). It is in conflict with a judgment of the Circuit Court of Appeals for the First Circuit, from which one judge dissented. *Davis v. Boston & Maine R. R. Co.,* April 14, 1937, - F.

(2d) -. An important question of constitutional law being involved, we granted certiorari.

The Social Security Act (Act of August 14, 1935, c. 531, 49 Stat. 620, 42 U. S. C., c. 7 (Supp.)) is divided into eleven separate titles, of which only Titles IX and III are so related to this case as to stand in need of summary.

The caption of Title IX is "Tax on Employers of Eight or More." Every employer (with stated exceptions) is to pay for each calendar year "an excise tax, with respect to having individuals in his employ", the tax to be measured by prescribed percentages of the total wages payable by the employer during the calendar year with respect to such employment. Section 901. One is not, however, an "employer" within the meaning of the act unless he employs eight persons or more. Section 907 (a). There are also other limitations of minor importance. The term "employment" too has its special definition, excluding agricultural labor, domestic service in a private home and some other smaller classes. Section 907 (c). The tax begins with the year 1936, and is payable for the first time on January 31, 1937. During the calendar year 1936 the rate is to be one per cent, during 1937 two per cent, and three per cent thereafter. The proceeds, when collected, go into the Treasury of the United States like internal-revenue collections generally. Section 905 (a). They are not earmarked in any way. In certain circumstances, however, credits are allowable. Section 902. If the taxpayer has made contributions to an unemployment fund under a state law, he may credit such contributions against the federal tax, provided, however, that the total credit allowed to any taxpayer shall not exceed 90 per centum of the tax against which it is credited, and provided also that the state law shall have been certified to the Secretary of the Treasury by the Social Security Board as satisfying certain minimum criteria.

Section 902. The provisions of Section 903 defining those criteria are stated in the margin.[1] Some of the conditions thus attached to the allowance of a credit are designed to give assurance that the state unemployment compensation law shall be one in substance as well as name. Others are designed to give assurance that the contributions shall be protected against loss after payment to the state. To this last end there are provisions that before a state law shall have the approval of the Board it must direct that the contributions to the state fund be paid over immediately to the Secretary of the Treasury to the credit of the "Unemployment Trust Fund." Section 904 establishing this fund is quoted below. **(2)** For the moment it is enough to say that the Fund is to be held by the Secretary of the Treasury, who is to invest in government securities any portion not required in his judgment to meet current withdrawals. He is authorized and directed to pay out of the Fund to any competent state agency such sums as it may duly requisition from the amount standing to its credit. Section 904 (f). Title III, which is also challenged as invalid, has the caption "Grants to States for Unemployment Compensation Administration." Under this title, certain sums of money are "authorized to be appropriated" for the purpose of assisting the states in the administration of their unemployment compensation laws, the maximum for the fiscal year ending June 30, 1936 to be $4,000,000, and $49,000,000 for each fiscal year thereafter. Section 301. No present appropriation is made to the extent of a single dollar. All that the title does is to authorize future appropriations. Actually only $2,250,000 of the $4,000,000 authorized was appropriated for 1936 (Act of Feb. 11, 1936, c. 49, 49 Stat. 1109, 1113) and only $29,000,000 of the $49,000,000 authorized for the following year. Act of June 22, 1936, c. 689, 49 Stat. 1597, 1605. The appropriations when made were not specifically out of the proceeds of the employment tax, but out of any moneys in the Treasury. Other sections of the title prescribe the method by which the payments are to be made to the state (Section 302) and also certain conditions to be established to the satisfaction of the Social Security Board before certifying the propriety of a payment to the Secretary of the Treasury. Section 303. They are designed to give assurance to the Federal

Government that the moneys granted by it will not be expended for purposes alien to the grant, and will be used in the administration of genuine unemployment compensation laws.

The assault on the statute proceeds on an extended front. Its assailants take the ground that the tax is not an excise; that it is not uniform throughout the United States as excises are required to be; that its exceptions are so many and arbitrary as to violate the Fifth Amendment; that its purpose was not revenue, but an unlawful invasion of the reserved powers of the states; and that the states in submitting to it have yielded to coercion and have abandoned governmental functions which they are not permitted to surrender.

The objections will be considered seriatim with such further explanation as may be necessary to make their meaning clear.

First: The tax, which is described in the statute as an excise, is laid with uniformity throughout the United States as a duty, an impost or an excise upon the relation of employment.

1. We are told that the relation of employment is one so essential to the pursuit of happiness that it may not be burdened with a tax. Appeal is made to history. From the precedents of colonial days we are supplied with illustrations of excises common in the colonies. They are said to have been bound up with the enjoyment of particular commodities. Appeal is also made to principle or the analysis of concepts. An excise, we are told, imports a tax upon a privilege; employment, it is said, is a right, not a privilege, from which it follows that employment is not subject to an excise. Neither the one appeal nor the other leads to the desired goal.

As to the argument from history: Doubtless there were many excises in colonial days and later that were associated, more or less intimately, with the enjoyment or the use of property. This would not prove, even if no others were then known, that the forms then accepted were not subject to enlargement. Cf. *Pensacola Telephone Co. v. Western Union Telegraph Co.,* 96 U. S. 1, 9; *In re Debs,* 158 U. S. 564, 591; *South Carolina v. United States,* 199 U. S. 437, 448, 449. But in truth other excises were known, and known since early times. Thus in 1695 (6 & 7 Wm. III, c. 6), Parliament passed an act which granted "to His Majesty certain Rates and Duties upon Marriage, Births and Burials", all for the purpose of "carrying on the War against France with Vigour." See *Opinion of the Justices,* 196 Mass. 602, 609. No commodity was affected there. The industry of counsel has supplied us with an apter illustration where the tax was not different in substance from the one now challenged as invalid. In 1777, before our Constitutional Convention, Parliament laid upon employers an annual "duty" of 21 shillings for "every male Servant" employed in stated forms of work. **(3)** Revenue Act of 1777, 17 George III, c. 39 **(4)** The point is made as a distinction that a tax upon the use of male servants was thought of as a tax upon a luxury. *Davis v. Boston & Maine R. R. Co.,* supra. It did not touch employments in husbandry or business. This is to throw over the argument that historically an excise is a tax upon the enjoyment of commodities. But the attempted distinction, whatever may be thought of its validity, is inapplicable to a statute of Virginia passed in 1780. There a tax of three pounds, six shillings and eight pence was to be paid for every male tithable above the age of twenty-one years (with stated exceptions), and a like tax for "every white servant whatsoever, except apprentices under the age of twenty one years." 10 Hening's Statutes of Virginia, p. 244. Our colonial forbears knew more about ways of taxing than some of their descendants seem to be willing to concede. **(5)**

The historical prop failing, the prop or fancied prop of principle remains. We learn that employment for lawful gain is a "natural" or "inherent" or "inalienable" right, and not a "privilege" at all. But natural rights, so called, are as much subject to taxation as rights of less importance. **(6)** An excise is not limited to vocations or activities that may be prohibited altogether. It is not limited to those that are the outcome of a franchise. It extends to vocations or activities pursued as of common right. What the individual does in the operation of a business is amenable to taxation just as much as what he owns, at all events if the classification is not tyrannical or arbitrary. "Business is as legitimate an object of the taxing powers as property." *City of Newton v. Atchison,* 31 Kan. 151, 154 (per Brewer, J.). Indeed, ownership itself, as we had occasion to point out the other day, is only a bundle of rights and privileges invested with a single name. *Henneford v. Silas Mason Co., Inc.,* March 29, 1937, - U. S. -. "A state is at liberty, if it pleases, to tax them all collectively, or to separate the faggots and lay the charge distributively." *Ibid.* Employment is a business relation, if not itself a business. It is a relation without which business could seldom be carried on effectively. The power to tax the activities and relations that constitute a calling considered as a unit is the power to tax any of them. The whole includes the parts. *Nashville C. & St. L. By. Co. v. Wallace,* 288 U. S. 249, 267, 268.

The subject matter of taxation open to the power of the Congress is as comprehensive as that open to the power of the states, though the method of apportionment may at times be different. "The Congress shall have power to lay and collect taxes, duties, imposts and excises". Art. 1, Sect. 8. If the tax is a direct one, it shall be apportioned according to the census or enumeration. If it is a duty, impost, or excise, it shall be uniform throughout the United States. Together these classes include every form of tax appropriate to sovereignty. Cf. *Burnet v. Brooks,* 288 U. S. 378, 403, 405; *Brushaber v. Union Pacific R.. R.. Co.,* 240 U. S. 1, 12.

Whether the tax is to be classified as an "excise" is in truth not of critical importance. If not that, it is an "impost" (*Pollock v. Farmers' Loan and Trust Co.,* 158 U. S. 601, 622, 625; *Pacific Insurance Co. v. Soule,* 7 Wall. 433, 445), or a "duty" (*Veazie Bank v. Fenno,* 8 Wall. 533, 546, 547; *Pollock v. Farmers' Loan and Trust Co.,* 157 U. S. 429, 570; *Knowlton v. Moore,* 178 U. S. 41, 46). A capitation or other "direct" tax it certainly is not. "Although there have been from time to time intimations that there might be some tax which was not a direct tax nor included under the words 'duties, imposts and excises,' such a tax for more than one hundred years of national existence has as yet remained undiscovered, not-withstanding the stress of particular circumstances has invited thorough investigation into sources of powers." *Pollock* v. Far*mers' Loan and Trust Co.,* 157 U. S. 429, 557. There is no departure from that thought in later cases, but rather a new emphasis of it. Thus, in *Thomas v. United States,* 192 U. S. 363, 370, it was said of the words "duties, imposts and excises" that "they were used comprehensively to cover customs and excise duties imposed on importation, consumption, manufacture and sale of certain commodities, privileges, particular business transactions, vocations, occupations and the like." At times taxpayers have contended that the Congress is without power to lay an excise on the enjoyment of a privilege created by state law. The contention has been put aside as baseless. Congress may tax the transmission of property by inheritance or will, though the states and not Congress have created the privilege of succession. *Knowlton v. Moore, supra,* p. 58. Congress may tax the enjoyment of a corporate franchise, though a state and notCongress has brought the franchise into being. *Flint v. Stone Tracy Co.,* 220 U. S. 108, 155. The statute books of the states are strewn with illustrations of taxes laid on occupations pursued of common right. **(7)** We find no basis for a holding that the power in that regard which belongs by accepted practice to the legislatures of the states, has been denied by the Constitution to the Congress of the nation.

2. The tax being an excise, its imposition must conform to the canon of uniformity. There has been no departure from this requirement. According to the settled doctrine the uniformity exacted is geographical, not intrinsic. *Knowlton v. Moore, supra,* p. 83; *Flint* v. *Stone Tracy Co., supra,* p. 158; *Billings v. United States,* 232 U. S. 261, 282; *Stellwagen* v. *Clum,* 245 U. S. 605, 613; *LaBelle Iron Works v. United States,* 256 U. S. 377, 392; *Poe v. Seaborn,* 282 U. S. 101, 117; *Wright v. Vinton Branch Mountain Trust Bank,* March 29, 1937, - U. S. -. "The rule of liability shall be

the same in all parts of the United States." *Florida v. Mellon*, 273 U. S. 12, 17.

Second: The excise is not invalid under the provisions of the Fifth Amendment by force of its exemptions.

The statute does not apply, as we have seen, to employers of less than eight. It does not apply to agricultural labor, or domestic service in a private home or to some other classes of less importance. Petitioner contends that the effect of these restrictions is an arbitrary discrimination vitiating the tax.

The Fifth Amendment unlike the Fourteenth has no equal protection clause. *LaBelle Iron Works v. United States, supra; Brushaber v. Union Pacific R.. R. Co., supra,* p. 24. But even the states, thought subject to such a clause, are not confined to a formula of rigid uniformity in framing measures of taxation. *Swiss Oil Corp. v. Shanks,* 273 U. S. 407, 413. They may tax some kinds of property at one rate, and others at another, and exempt others altogether. *Bell's Gap R. R.. Co. v. Pennsylvania*, 134 U. S. 232; *Stebbins v. Riley*, 268 U. S. 137, 142; *Ohio Oil Co. v. Conway*, 281 U. S. 146, 150. They may lay an excise on the operations of a particular kind of business, and exempt some other kind of business closely akin thereto. *Quong Wing v. Kirkendall,* 223 U. S. 59, 62; *American Sugar Refining Co. v. Louisiana*, 179 U. S. 89, 94; *Armour Packing Co. v. Lacy*, 200 U. S. 226, 235; *Brown-Forman Co. v. Kentucky*, 217 U. S. 563, 573; *Heisler v. Thomas Colliery Co.*, 260 U. S. 245, 255; *State Board of Tax Commissioners v. Jackson*, 283 U. S. 527, 537, 538. If this latitude of judgment is lawful for the states, it is lawful, a fortiori, in legislation by the Congress, which is subject to restraints less narrow and confining. *Quong Wing v. Kirkendall, supra.*

The classifications and exemptions directed by the statute now in controversy have support in considerations of policy and practical convenience that cannot be condemned as arbitrary. The classifications and exemptions would therefore be upheld if they had been adopted by a state and the provisions of the Fourteenth Amendment were invoked to annul them. This is held in two cases passed upon today in which precisely the same provisions were the subject of attack, the provisions being, contained in the Unemployment Compensation Law of the State of Alabama. *Carmichael v. Southern Coal & Coke Co.,* No. 724, - U. S. -, and *Carmichael v. Gulf States Paper Corp.,* No. 797, - U. S. -. The opinion rendered in those cases covers the ground fully. It would be useless to repeat the argument. The act of Congress is therefore valid, so far at least as its system of exemptions is concerned, and this though we assume that discrimination, if gross enough, is equivalent to confiscation and subject under the Fifth Amendment to challenge and annulment.

Third: The excise is not void as involving the coercion of the States in contravention of the Tenth Amendment or of restrictions implicit in our federal form of government.

The proceeds of the excise when collected are paid into the Treasury at Washington, and thereafter are subject to appropriation like public moneys generally. *Cincinnati Soap Co. v. United States,* May 3, 1937, - U. S. -. No presumption can be indulged that they will be misapplied or wasted. **(8)** Even if they were collected in the hope or expectation that some other and collateral good would be furthered as an incident, that without more would not make the act invalid. *Sonzinsky v. United States,* March 29, 1937, - U. S. -. This indeed is hardly questioned. The case for the petitioner is built on the contention that here an ulterior aim is wrought into the very structure of the act, and what is even more important that the aim is not only ulterior, but essentially unlawful. In particular, the 90 per cent credit is relied upon as supporting that conclusion. But before the statute succumbs to an assault upon these lines, two propositions must be made out by the assailant. *Cincinnati Soap Co. v. United States, supra.* There must be a showing in the first place that separated from the credit the revenue provisions are incapable of standing by themselves. There must be a showing in the second place that the tax and the credit in combination are weapons of coercion, destroying or impairing the autonomy of the states. The truth of each proposition being essential to the success of the assault, we pass for convenience to a consideration of the second, without pausing to inquire whether there has been a demonstration of the first.

To draw the line intelligently between duress and inducement there is need to remind ourselves of facts as to the problem of unemployment that are now matters of common knowledge. *West Coast Hotel Co. v. Parrish,* March 29, 1937, - U. S. -. The relevant statistics are gathered in the brief of counsel for the Government. Of the many available figures a few only will be mentioned. During the years 1929 to 1936, when the country was passing through a cyclical depression, the number of the unemployed mounted to unprecedented heights. Often the average was more than 10 million; at times a peak was attained of 16 million or more. Disaster to the breadwinner meant disaster to dependents. Accordingly the roll of the unemployed, itself formidable enough, was only a partial roll of the destitute or needy. The fact developed quickly that the states were unable to give the requisite relief. The problem had become national in area and dimensions. There was need of help from the nation if the people were not to starve. It is too late today for the argument to be heard with tolerance that in a crisis so extreme the use of the moneys of the nation to relieve the unemployed and their dependents is a use for any purpose narrower than the promotion of the general welfare. Cf. *United States v. Butler,* 297 U. S. 1, 65, 66, *Helvering v. Davis,* decided herewith. The nation responded to the call of the distressed. Between January 1, 1933 and July 1, 1936, the states (according to statistics submitted by the Government) incurred obligations of $689,291,802 for emergency relief; local subdivisions an additional $775,675,366. In the same period the obligations for emergency relief incurred by the national government were $2,929,307,125, or twice the obligations of states and local agencies combined. According to the President's budget message for the fiscal year 1938, the national government expended for public works and unemployment relief for the three fiscal years 1934, 1935, and 1936, the stupendous total of $8,681,000,000. The **parens patriae** has many reasons-fiscal and economic as well as social and moral-for planning to mitigate disasters that bring these burdens in their train.

In the presence of this urgent need for some remedial expedient, the question is to be answered whether the expedient adopted has overleapt the bounds of power. The assailants of the statute say that its dominant end and aim is to drive the state legislatures under the whip of economic pressure into the enactment of unemployment compensation laws at the bidding of the central government. Supporters of the statute say that its operation is not constraint, but the creation of a larger freedom, the states and the nation joining in a cooperative endeavor to avert a common evil. Before Congress acted, unemployment compensation insurance was still, for the most part, a project and no more. Wisconsin was the pioneer. Her statute was adopted in 1931. At times bills for such insurance were introduced elsewhere, but they did not reach the stage of law. In 1935 four states (California, Massachusetts, New Hampshire and New York) passed unemployment laws on the eve of the adoption of the Social Security Act, and two others did likewise after the federal act and later in the year. The statutes differed to some extent in type, but were directed to a common end. In 1936, twenty-eight other states fell in line, and eight more the present year. But if states had been holding back before the passage of the federal law, inaction was not owing, for the most part, to the lack of sympathetic interest. Many held back through alarm lest in laying such a toll upon their industries, they would place themselves in a position of economic disadvantage as compared with neighbors or competitors. See House Report, No. 615, 74th Congress, 1st session, p. 8; Senate Report, No. 628, 74th Congress, 1st session, p. 11. **(9)** Two consequences ensued. One was that the freedom of a state to contribute its fair share to the solution of a national problem was paralyzed by fear. The other was that in so far as

90

there was failure by the states to contribute relief according to the measure of their capacity, a disproportionate burden, and a mountainous one, was laid upon the resources of the Government of the nation.

The Social Security Act is an attempt to find a method by which all these public agencies may work together to a common end. Every dollar of the new taxes will continue in all likelihood to be used and needed by the nation as long as states are unwilling, whether through timidity or for other motives, to do what can be done at home. At least the inference is permissible that Congress so believed, though retaining undiminished freedom to spend the money as it pleased. On the other hand fulfillment of the home duty will be lightened and encouraged by crediting the taxpayer upon his account with the Treasury of the nation to the extent that his contributions under the laws of the locality have simplified or diminished the problem of relief and the probable demand upon the resources of the fisc. Duplicated taxes, or burdens that approach them, are recognized hardships that government, state or national, may properly avoid. *Henneford v. Silas Mason Co., Inc., supra; Kidd v. Alabama,* 188 U. S. 730, 732; *Watson v. State Comptroller,* 254 U. S. 122, 125.

If Congress believed that the general welfare would better be promoted by relief through local units than by the system then in vogue, the cooperating localities ought not in all fairness to pay a second time.

Who then is coerced through the operation of this statute? Not the taxpayer. He pays in fulfillment of the mandate of the local legislature. Not the state. Even now she does not offer a suggestion that in passing the unemployment law she was affected by duress. See *Carmichael v. Southern Coal & Coke Co., supra; Carmichael v. Gulf States Paper Corp., supra.* For all that appears she is satisfied with her choice, and would be sorely disappointed if it were now to be annulled. The difficulty with the petitioner's contention is that it confuses motive with coercion.

"Every tax is in some measure regulatory. To some extent it interposes an economic impediment to the activity taxed as compared with others not taxed." *Sonzinsky v. United States, supra.* In like manner every rebate from a tax when conditioned upon conduct is in some measure a temptation. But to hold that motive or temptation is equivalent to coercion is to plunge the law in endless difficulties. The outcome of such a doctrine is the acceptance of a philosophical determinism by which choice becomes impossible. Till now the law has been guided by a robust common sense which assumes the freedom of the will as a working hypothesis in the solution of its problems. The wisdom of the hypothesis has illustration in this case. Nothing in the case suggests the exertion of a power akin to undue influence, if we assume that such a concept can ever be applied with fitness to the relations between state and nation. Even on that assumption the location of the point at which pressure turns into compulsion, and ceases to be inducement, would be a question of degree, at times, perhaps, of fact. The point had not been reached when Alabama made her choice. We cannot say that she was acting, not of her unfettered will but under the strain of a persuasion equivalent to undue influence, when she chose to have relief administered under laws of her own making, by agents of her own selection, instead of under federal laws, administered by federal officers, with all the ensuing evils, at least to many minds, of federal patronage and power. There would be a strange irony, indeed, if her choice were now to be annulled on the basis of an assumed duress in the enactment of a statute which her courts have accepted as a true expression of her will. *Beeland Wholesale Co. v. Kaufman, supra.* We think the choice must stand.

In ruling as we do, we leave many questions open. We do not say that a tax is valid, when imposed by act of Congress, if it is laid upon the condition that a state may escape its operation through the adoption of a statute unrelated in subject matter to activities fairly within the scope of national policy and power. No such question is before us. In the tender of this credit Congress does not intrude upon fields foreign to its function. The purpose of its intervention, as we have shown, is to safeguard its own treasury and as an incident to that protection to place the states upon a footing of equal opportunity. Drains upon its own resources are to be checked; obstructions to the freedom of the states are to be leveled. It is one thing to impose a tax dependent upon the conduct of the taxpayers, or of the state in which they live, where the conduct to be stimulated or discouraged is unrelated to the fiscal need subserved by the tax in its normal operation, or to any other end legitimately national. The *Child Labor Tax Case,* 259 U. S. 20, and *Hill v. Wallace,* 259 U. S. 44, were decided in the belief that the statutes there condemned were exposed to that reproach. *Cf. United States v. Constantine,* 296 U. S. 287. It is quite another thing to say that a tax will be abated upon the doing of an act that will satisfy the fiscal need, the tax and the alternative being approximate equivalents. In such circumstances, if in no others, inducement or persuasion does not go beyond the bounds of power. We do not fix the outermost line. Enough for present purposes that wherever the line may be, this statute is within it.

Definition more precise must abide the wisdom of the future. *Florida v. Mellon*, 273 U. S. 12, supplies us with a precedent, if precedent be needed. What was in controversy there was section 301 of the Revenue Act of 1926, which imposes a tax upon the transfer of a decedent's estate, while at the same time permitting credit, not exceeding 80 per cent, for "the amount of any estate, inheritance, legacy or succession taxes actually paid to any State or Territory". Florida challenged that provision as unlawful. Florida had no inheritance taxes and alleged that under its constitution it could not levy any. 273 U. S. 12, 15. Indeed, by abolishing inheritance taxes, it had hoped to induce wealthy persons to become its citizens. See 67 Cong. Rec., Part 1, pp. 735, 752. It argued at our bar that "the Estate Tax provision was not passed for the purpose of raising federal revenue" (273 U. S. 12, 14), but rather "to coerce States into adopting estate or inheritance tax laws." 273 U. S. 12, 13. In fact, as a result of the 80 per cent credit, material changes of such laws were made in 36 states. **(10)** In the face of that attack we upheld the act as valid.

Cf. *Massachusetts v. Mellon,* 262 U. S. 447, 482; also Act of August 5, 1861, c. 45, 12 Stat. 292; Act of May 13, 1862, c. 66, 12 Stat. 384.

United States v. Butler, supra, is cited by petitioner as a decision to the contrary. There a tax was imposed on processors of farm products, the proceeds to be paid to farmers who would reduce their acreage and crops under agreements with the Secretary of Agriculture, the plan of the act being to increase the prices of certain farm products by decreasing, the quantities produced. The court held (1) that the so-called tax was not a true one (pp. 56, 61), the proceeds being earmarked for the benefit of farmers complying with the prescribed conditions, (2) that there was an attempt to regulate production without the consent of the state in which production was affected, and (3) that the payments to farmers were coupled with coercive contracts (p. 73), unlawful in their aim and oppressive in their consequences. The decision was by a divided court, a minority taking the view that the objections were untenable. None of them is applicable to the situation here developed.

(a) The proceeds of the tax in controversy are not earmarked for a special group.

(b) The unemployment compensation law which is a condition of the credit has had the approval of the state and could not be a law without it.

(c) The condition is not linked to an irrevocable agreement, for the state at its pleasure may repeal its unemployment law (Section 903 (a) (6)), terminate the credit, and place itself where it was before the credit was accepted.

(d) The condition is not directed to the attainment of an unlawful end, but to an end, the relief of unemployment, for which nation and state may lawfully cooperate.

Fourth: The statute does not call for a surrender by the states of powers essential to their quasi-sovereign existence.

Argument to the contrary has its source in two sections of the act. One section (903 **(11)**) defines the minimum criteria to which a state compensation system is required to conform if it is to be accepted by the Board as the basis for a credit. The other section (904 **(12)**) rounds out the requirement with complementary rights and duties. Not all the criteria or their incidents are challenged as unlawful. We will speak of them first generally, and then more specifically in so far as they are questioned.

A credit to taxpayers for payments made to a State under a state unemployment law will be manifestly futile in the absence of some assurance that the law leading to the credit is in truth what it professes to be. An unemployment law framed in such a way that the unemployed who look to it will be deprived of reasonable protection is one in name and nothing more. What is basic and essential may be assured by suitable conditions. The terms embodied in these sections are directed to that end. A wide range of judgment is given to the several states as to the particular type of statute to be spread upon their books. For anything to the contrary in the provisions of this act they may use the pooled unemployment form, which is in effect with variations in Alabama, California, Michigan, New York, and elsewhere. They may establish a system of merit ratings applicable at once or to go into effect later on the basis of subsequent experience. Cf. Sections 909, 910. They may provide for employee contributions as in Alabama and California, or put the entire burden upon the employer as in New York. They may choose a system of unemployment reserve accounts by which an employer is permitted after his reserve has accumulated to contribute at a reduced rate or even not at all.

This is the system which had its origin in Wisconsin. What they may not do, if they would earn the credit, is to depart from those standards which in the judgment of Congress are to be ranked as fundamental. Even if opinion may differ as to the fundamental quality of one or more of the conditions, the difference will not avail to vitiate the statute. In determining essentials Congress must have the benefit of a fair margin of discretion. One cannot say with reason that this margin has been exceeded, or that the basic standards have been determined in any arbitrary fashion. In the event that some particular condition shall be found to be too uncertain to be capable of enforcement, it may be severed from the others, and what is left will still be valid.

We are to keep in mind steadily that the conditions to be approved by the Board as the basis for a credit are not provisions of a contract, but terms of a statute, which may be altered or repealed. Section 903 (a) (6). The state does not bind itself to keep the law in force. It does not even bind itself that the moneys paid into the federal fund will be kept there indefinitely or for any stated time. On the contrary, the Secretary of the Treasury will honor a requisition for the whole or any part of the deposit in the fund whenever one is made by the appropriate officials. The only consequence of the repeal or excessive amendment of the statute, or the expenditure of the money, when requisitioned, for other than compensation uses or administrative expenses, is that approval of the law will end, and with it the allowance of a credit, upon notice to the state agency and an opportunity for hearing. Section 903 (b)(c).

These basic considerations are in truth a solvent of the problem. Subjected to their test, the several objections on the score of abdication are found to be unreal.

Thus, the argument is made that by force of an agreement the moneys when withdrawn must be "paid through public employment offices in the State or through such other agencies as the Board may approve." Section 903 (a) (1). But in truth there is no agreement as to the method of disbursement. There is only a condition which the state is free at pleasure to disregard or to fulfill. Moreover, approval is not requisite if public employment offices are made the disbursing instruments. Approval is to be a check upon resort to "other agencies" that may, perchance, be irresponsible. A state looking for a credit must give assurance that her system has been organized upon a base of rationality.

There is argument again that the moneys when withdrawn are to be devoted to specific uses, the relief of unemployment, and that by agreement for such payment the quasi-sovereign position of the state has been impaired, if not abandoned. But again there is confusion between promise and condition. Alabama is still free, without breach of an agreement, to change her system over night. No officer or agency of the national Government can force a compensation law upon her or keep it in existence. No officer or agency of that Government, either by suit or other means, can supervise or control the application of the payments.

Finally and chiefly, abdication is supposed to follow from section 904 of the statute and the parts of section 903 that are complementary thereto. Section 903 (a) (3). By these the Secretary of the Treasury is authorized and directed to receive and hold in the Unemployment Trust Fund all moneys deposited therein by a state agency for a state unemployment fund and to invest in obligations of the United States such portion of the Fund as is not in his judgment required to meet current withdrawals. We are told that Alabama in consenting to that deposit has renounced the plenitude of power inherent in her statehood.

The same pervasive misconception is in evidence again. All that the state has done is to say in effect through the enactment of a statute that her agents shall be authorized to deposit the unemployment tax receipts in the Treasury at Washington. Alabama Unemployment Act of September 14, 1935, section 10 (i). The statute may be repealed. Section 903 (a) (6). The consent may be revoked. The deposits may be withdrawn. The moment the state commission gives notice to the depositary that it would like the moneys back, the Treasurer will return them. To find state destruction there is to find it almost anywhere. With nearly as much reason one might say that a state abdicates its functions when it places the state moneys on deposit in a national bank.

There are very good reasons of fiscal and governmental policy why a State should be willing to make the Secretary of the Treasury the custodian of the fund. His possession of the money and his control of investments will be an assurance of stability and safety in times of stress and strain. A report of the Ways and Means Committee of the House of Representatives, quoted in the margin, develops the situation clearly. **(13)** Nor is there risk of loss or waste. The credit of the Treasury is at all times back of the deposit, with the result that the right of withdrawal will be unaffected by the fate of any intermediate investments, just as if a checking account in the usual form had been opened in a bank.

The inference of abdication thus dissolves in thinnest air when the deposit is conceived of as dependent upon a statutory consent, and not upon a contract effective to create a duty. By this we do not intimate that the conclusion would be different if a contract were discovered. Even sovereigns may contract without derogating from their sovereignty. *Perry v. United States,* 294 U. S. 330, 353; 1 Oppenheim, International Law, 4th ed., 493, 494; Hall, International Law, 8th ed., 107; 2 Hyde, International Law, 489. The states are at liberty, upon obtaining the consent of Congress, to make agreements with one another. Constitution, Art. 1, section 10, par. 3. *Poole V. Fleeger,* 11 Pet. 185, 209; *Rhode Island* v. *Massachusetts,* 12 Pet. 657, 725. We find no room for doubt that they may do the like with Congress if the essence of their statehood is maintained without impairment. **(14)** Alabama is seeking and obtaining a credit of many millions in favor of her citizens out of the Treasury of the nation. Nowhere in our scheme of government-in the limitations express or implied of our federal constitution-do we find that she is prohibited from assenting to conditions that will assure a fair and just requital for benefits received. But we will not labor the point further. An unreal prohibition directed to an unreal agreement will not vitiate an act of Congress, and cause it to collapse in ruin.

Fifth: Title III of the act is separable from Title IX, and its validity is not at issue.

The essential provisions of that title have been stated in the opinion. As already pointed out, the title does not appropriate a dollar of the public moneys. It does no more than authorize appropriations to be made in the future for the purpose of assisting states in the administration of their laws, if Congress shall decide that appropriations are desirable. The title might be expunged, and Title IX would stand intact. Without a severability clause we should still be led to that conclusion. The presence of such a clause (Section 1103) makes the conclusion even clearer. *Williams v. Standard Oil Co.,* 278 U. S. 235, 242; *Utah Power & Light Co.* v. *Pfost,* 286 U. S. 165, 184; *Carter v. Carter Coal Co.,* 298 U. S. 238, 312.

The judgment is ***Affirmed.***

Separate opinion of Mr. Justice McREYNOLDS.

That portion of the Social Security legislation here under consideration, I think, exceeds the power granted to Congress. It unduly interferes with the orderly government of the state by her own people and otherwise offends the Federal Constitution.

In Texas v. White (1869) 7 Wall. 700, 725, 19 L.Ed. 227, a cause of momentous importance, this Court, through Chief Justice Chase, declared—

'But the perpetuity and indissolubility of the Union, by no means implies the loss of distinct and individual existence, or of the right of self-government by the States. Under the Articles of Confederation each State retained its sovereignty, freedom, and independence, and every power, jurisdiction, and right not expressly delegated to the United States. Under the Constitution, though the powers of the States were much restricted, still, all powers not delegated to the United States, nor prohibited to the

States, are reserved to the States respectively, or to the people. And we have already had occasion to remark at this term, that 'the people of each State compose a State, having its own government, and endowed with all the functions essential to separate and independent existence,' and that 'without the States in union, there could be no such political body as the United States.' (Lane County v. Oregon, 7 Wall. 71, 76, 19 L.Ed. 101). Not only, therefore, can there be no loss of separate and independent autonomy to the States, through their union under the Constitution, but it may be not unreasonably said that the preservation of the States, and the maintenance of their governments, are as much within the design and care of the Constitution as the preservation of the Union and the maintenance of the National Government. The Constitution, in all its provisions, looks to an indestructible Union, composed of indestructible States.'

The doctrine thus announced and often repeated, I had supposed was firmly established. Apparently the states remained really free to exercise governmental powers, not delegated or prohibited, without interference by the federal government through threats of punitive measures or offers of seductive favors. Unfortunately, the decision just announced opens the way for practical annihilation of this theory; and no cloud of words or ostentatious parade of irrelevant statistics should be permitted to obscure that fact.

The invalidity also the destructive tendency of legislation like the act before us were forcefully pointed out by President Franklin Pierce in a veto message sent to the Senate May 3, 1854.1 He was a scholarly lawyer of distinction and enjoyed the advice and counsel of a rarely able Attorney General—Caleb Cushing of Massachusetts. This message considers with unusual lucidity points here specially important. I venture to set out pertinent portions of it which must appeal to all who continue to respect both the letter and spirit of our great charter.

'To the Senate of the United States:

'The bill entitled 'An Act making a grant of public lands to the several States for the benefit of indigent insane persons,' which was presented to me on the 27th ultimo, has been maturely considered, and is returned to the Senate, the House in which it originated, with a statement of the objections which have required me to withhold from it may approval. ...

'If in presenting my objections to this bill I should say more than strictly belongs to the measure or is required for the discharge of my official obligation, let it be attributed to a sincere desire to justify my act before those whose good opinion I so highly value and to that earnestness which springs from my deliberate conviction that a strict adherence to the terms and purposes of the federal compact offers the best, if not the only, security for the preservation of our blessed inheritance of representative liberty.

'The bill provides in substance:

'First. That 10,000,000 acres of land be granted to the several States, to be apportioned among them in the compound ratio of the geographical area and representation of said States in the House of Representatives.

'Second. That wherever there are public lands in a State subject to sale at the regular price of private entry, the proportion of said 10,000,000 acres falling to such State shall be selected from such lands within it, and that to the States in which there are no such public lands land scrip shall be issued to the amount of their distributive shares, respectively, said scrip not to be entered by said States, but to be sold by them and subject to entry by their assignees: Provided, That none of it shall be sold at less than $1 per acre, under penalty of forfeiture of the same to the United States.

'Third. That the expenses of the management and superintendence of said lands and of the moneys received therefrom shall be paid by the States to which they may belong out of the treasury of said States.

'Fourth. That the gross proceeds of the sales of such lands or land scrip so granted shall be invested by the several States in safe stocks, to constitute a perpetual fund, the principal of which shall remain forever undiminished, and the interest to be appropriated to the maintenance of the indigent insane within the several States.

'Fifth. That annual returns of lands or scrip sold shall be made by the States to the Secretary of the Interior, and the whole grant be subject to certain conditions and limitations prescribed in the bill, to be assented to by legislative acts of said States.

'This bill therefore proposes that the Federal Government shall make provision to the amount of the value of 10,000,000 acres of land for an eleemosynary object within the several States, to be administered by the political authority of the same; and it presents at the threshold the question whether any such act on the part of the Federal Government is warranted and sanctioned by the Constitution, the provisions and principles of which are to be protected and sustained as a first and paramount duty.

'It can not be questioned that if Congress has power to make provision for the indigent insane without the limits of this District it has the same power to provide for the indigent who are not insane, and thus to transfer to the Federal Government the charge of all the poor in all the States. It has the same power to provide hospitals and other local establishments for the care and cure of every species of human infirmity, and thus to assume all that duty of either public philanthropy or public necessity to the dependent, the orphan, the sick, or the needy which is now discharged by the States themselves or by corporate institutions or private endowments existing under the legislation of the States.

The whole field of public beneficence is thrown open to the care and culture of the Federal Government. Generous impulses no longer encounter the limitations and control of our imperious fundamental law; for however worthy may be the present object in itself, it is only one of a class. It is not exclusively worthy of benevolent regard. Whatever considerations dictate sympathy for this particular object apply in like manner, if not in the same degree, to idiocy, to physical disease, to extreme destitution. If Congress may and ought to provide for any one of these objects, it may and ought to provide for them all. And if it be done in this case, what answer shall be given when Congress shall be called upon, as it doubtless will be, to pursue a similar course of legislation in the others? It will obviously be vain to reply that the object is worthy, but that the application has taken a wrong direction. The power will have been deliberately assumed, the general obligation will by this act have been acknowledged, and the question of means and expediency will alone be left for consideration. The decision upon the principle in any one case determines it for the whole class. The question presented, therefore, clearly is upon the constitutionality and propriety of the Federal Government assuming to enter into a novel and vast field of legislation, namely, that of providing for the care and support of all those among the people of the United States who by any form of calamity become fit objects of public philanthropy.

'I readily and, I trust, feelingly acknowledge the duty incumbent on us all as men and citizens, and as among the highest and holiest of our duties, to provide for those who, in the mysterious order of Providence, are subject to want and to disease of body or mind; but I can not find any authority in the Constitution for making the Federal Government the great almoner of public charity throughout the United States. To do so would, in my judgment, be contrary to the letter and spirit of the Constitution and subversive of the whole theory upon which the Union of these States is founded. And if it were admissible to contemplate the exercise of this power for any object whatever, I can not avoid the belief that it would in the end be prejudicial rather than beneficial in the noble offices of charity to have the charge of them transferred from the States to the Federal Government. Are we not too prone to forget that the Federal Union is the creature of the States, not they of the Federal Union? We were the inhabitants of colonies distinct in local government one from the other before the Revolution. By the Revolution the colonies each became an independent State. They achieved that independence and secured its recognition by the agency of a consulting body, which, from being an assembly of the ministers of distinct sovereignties instructed to agree to no form of government which did not leave the domestic concerns of each State to itself, was appropriately denominated a Congress. When, having tried the experiment of the Confederation, they resolved to change that for the present Federal Union, and thus to confer on the Federal Government more ample authority, they scrupulously measured such of the functions of their cherished sovereignty as they chose to delegate to the General Government. With this aim and to this end the fathers of the Republic framed the Constitution, in and by which the independent and sovereign States united themselves for certain specified objects and purposes, and for those only, leaving all powers not therein set forth as conferred on one or another of the three great departments—the legislative, the executive, and the judicial—indubitably with the States. And when the people of the several States had in their State conventions, and thus alone, given effect and force to the Constitution, not content that any doubt should in future arise as to the scope and character of this act, they ingrafted thereon the explicit declaration that 'the powers not delegated to the United States by the Constitution nor prohibited by it to the

States are reserved to the States respectively or to the people.'

'Can it be controverted that the great mass of the business of Government—that involved in the social relations, the internal arrangements of the body politic, the mental and moral culture of men, the development of local resources of wealth, the punishment of crimes in general, the preservation of order, the relief of the needy or otherwise unfortunate members of society—did in practice remain with the States; that none of these objects of local concern are by the Constitution expressly or impliedly prohibited to the States, and that none of them are by any express language of the Constitution transferred to the United States? Can it be claimed that any of these functions of local administration and legislation are vested in the Federal Government by any implication? I have never found anything in the Constitution which is susceptible of such a construction. No one of the enumerated powers touches the subject or has even a remote analogy to it. The powers conferred upon the United States have reference to federal relations, or to the means of accomplishing or executing things of federal relation. So also of the same character are the powers taken away from the States by enumeration. In either case the powers granted and the powers restricted were so granted or so restricted only where it was requisite for the maintenance of peace and harmony between the States or for the purpose of protecting their common interests and defending their common sovereignty against aggression from abroad or insurrection at home.

'I shall not discuss at length the question of power sometimes claimed for the General Government under the clause of the eighth section of the Constitution, which gives Congress the power 'to lay and collect taxes, duties, imposts, and excises, to pay debts and provide for the common defense and general welfare of the United States,' because if it has not already been settled upon sound reason and authority it never will be. I take the received and just construction of that article, as if written to lay and collect taxes, duties, imposts, and excises in order to pay the debts and in order to provide for the common defense and general welfare. It is not a substantive general power to provide for the welfare of the United States, but is a limitation on the grant of power to raise money by taxes, duties, and imposts. If it were otherwise, all the rest of the Constitution, consisting of carefully enumerated and cautiously guarded grants of specific powers, would have been useless, if not delusive. It would be impossible in that view to escape from the conclusion that these were inserted only to mislead for the present, and, instead of enlightening and defining the pathway of the future, in involve its action in the mazes of doubtful construction. Such a conclusion the character of the men who framed that sacred instrument will never permit us to form. Indeed, to suppose it susceptible of any other construction would be to consign all the rights of the States and of the people of the States to the mere discretion of Congress, and thus to clothe the Federal Government with authority to control the sovereign States, by which they would have been dwarfed into provinces or departments and all sovereignty vested in an absolute consolidated central power, against which the spirit of liberty has so often and in so many countries struggled in vain.

'In my judgment you can not by tributes to humanity make any adequate compensation for the wrong you would inflict by removing the sources of power and political action from those who are to be thereby affected. If the time shall ever arrive when, for an object appealing, however strongly, to our sympathies, the dignity of the States shall bow to the dictation of Congress by conforming their legislation thereto, when the power and majesty and honor of those who created shall become subordinate to the thing of their creation, I but feebly utter my apprehensions when I express my firm conviction that we shall see 'the beginning of the end.'

'Fortunately, we are not left in doubt as to the purpose of the Constitution any more than as to its express language, for although the history of its formation, as recorded in the Madison Papers, shows that the Federal Government in its present form emerged from the conflict of opposing influences which have continued to divide statesmen from that day to this, yet the rule of clearly defined powers and of strict construction presided over the actual conclusion and subsequent adoption of the Constitution. President Madison, in the Federalist, says:

"The powers delegated to the proposed Constitution are few and defined. Those which are to remain in the State governments are numerous and indefinite. ...Its (the General Government's) jurisdiction extends to certain enumerated objects only, and leaves to the several States a residuary and inviolable sovereignty over all other objects.' 'In the same spirit President Jefferson invokes 'the support of the State governments in all their rights as the most competent administrations for our domestic concerns and the surest bulwarks against anti-republican tendencies;' and President Jackson said that our true strength and wisdom are not promoted by invasions of the rights and powers of the several States, but that, on the contrary, they consist 'not in binding the States more closely to the center, but in leaving each more unobstructed in its proper orbit.'

'The framers of the Constitution, in refusing to confer on the Federal Government any jurisdiction over these purely local objects, in my judgment manifested a wise forecast and broad comprehension of the true interests of these objects themselves. It is clear that public charities Within the States can be efficiently administered only by their authority. The bill before me concedes this, for it does not commit the funds it provides to the administration of any other authority.

'I can not but repeat what I have before expressed, that if the several States, many of which have already laid the foundation of munificent establishments of local beneficence, and nearly all of which are proceeding to establish them, shall be led to suppose, as, should this bill become a law, they will be, that Congress is to make provision for such objects the fountains of charity will be dried up at home and the several States instead of bestowing their own means on the social wants of their own people may themselves, through the strong temptation which appeals to states as to individuals, become humble suppliants for the bounty of the Federal Government, reversing their true relations to this Union. ...

'I have been unable to discover any distinction on constitutional grounds or grounds of expediency between an appropriation of $10,000,000 directly from the money in the Treasury for the object contemplated and the appropriation of lands presented for my sanction, and yet I can not doubt that if the bill proposed $10,000,000 from the Treasury of the United States for the support of the indigent insane in the several States that the constitutional question involved in the act would have attracted forcibly the attention of Congress.

'I respectfully submit that in a constitutional point of view it is wholly immaterial whether the appropriation be in money or in land. ...

'To assume that the public lands are applicable to ordinary State objects, whether of public structures, police, charity, or expenses of State administration, would be to disregard to the amount of the value of the public lands all the limitations of the Constitution and confound to that extent all distinctions between the rights and powers of the States and those of the United States; for if the public lands may be applied to the support of the poor, whether sane or insane, if the disposal of them and their proceeds be not subject to the ordinary limitations of the Constitution, then Congress possesses unqualified power to provide for expenditures in the States by means of the public lands, even to the degree of defraying the salaries of governors, judges, and all other expenses of the government and internal administration within the several States.

'The conclusion from the general survey of the whole subject is to my mind irresistible, and closes the question both of right and of expediency so far as regards the principle of the appropriation proposed in this bill. Would not the admission of such power in Congress to dispose of the public domain work the practical abrogation of some of the most important provisions of the Constitution? ... 'The general result at which I have arrived is the necessary consequence of those views of the relative rights, powers, and duties of the States and of the Federal Government which I have long entertained and often expressed and in reference to which my convictions do but increase in force with time and experience.'

No defense is offered for the legislation under review upon the basis of emergency. The hypothesis is that hereafter it will continuously benefit unemployed members of a class. Forever, so far as we can see, the states are expected to function under federal direction concerning an internal matter. By the sanction of this adventure, the door is open for progressive inauguration of others of like kind under which it can hardly be expected that the states will retain genuine independence of action. And without independent states a Federal Union as contemplated by the Constitution becomes impossible.

At the bar counsel asserted that under the present act the tax upon residents of Alabama during the first year will total $9,000,000. All would remain in the Federal Treasury but for the adoption by the state of measures agreeable to the National Board. If continued, these will bring relief from the payment of $8,000,000 to the United States.

Ordinarily, I must think, a denial that the challenged action of Congress and what has been done under it amount to coercion and impair freedom of government by the people of the state would be regarded as contrary to practical experience. Unquestionably our federate plan of government confronts an enlarged peril.

Separate opinion of Mr. Justice SUTHERLAND.

With most of what is said in the opinion just handed down, I concur. I agree that the pay roll tax levied is an excise within the power of Congress; that the devotion of not more than 90 per cent. of it to the credit of employers in states which require the payment of a similar tax under so-called unemployment-tax laws is not an unconstitutional use of the proceeds of the federal tax; that the provision making the adoption by the state of an unemployment law of a specified character a condition precedent to the credit of the tax does not render the law invalid. I agree that the states are not coerced by the federal legislation into adopting unemployment legislation. The provisions of the federal law may operate to induce the state to pass an employment law if it regards such action to be in its interest. But that is not coercion. If the act stopped here, I should accept the conclusion of the court that the legislation is not unconstitutional.

But the question with which I have difficulty is whether the administrative provisions of the act invade the governmental administrative powers of the several states reserved by the Tenth Amendment. A state may enter into contracts; but a state cannot, by contract or statute, surrender the execution, or a share in the execution, of any of its governmental powers either to a sister state or to the federal government, any more than the federal government can surrender the control of any of its governmental powers to a foreign nation. The power to tax is vital and fundamental, and, in the highest degree, governmental in character. Without it, the state could not exist. Fundamental also,

110

and no less important, is the governmental power to expend the moneys realized from taxation, and exclusively to administer the laws in respect of the character of the tax and the methods of laying and collecting it and expending the proceeds.

The people of the United States, by their Constitution, have affirmed a division of internal governmental powers between the federal government and the governments of the several states committing to the first its powers by express grant and necessary implication; to the latter, or to the people, by reservation, 'the powers not delegated to the United States by the Constitution, nor prohibited by it to the States.' The Constitution thus affirms the complete supremacy and independence of the state within the field of its powers. Carter v. Carter Coal Co., 298 U.S. 238, 295, 56 S.Ct. 855, 865, 80 L.Ed. 1160. The federal government has no more authority to invade that field than the state has to invade the exclusive field of national governmental powers; for, in the oft repeated words of this court in Texas v. White, 7 Wall. 700, 725, 19 L.Ed. 227, 'the preservation of the States, and the maintenance of their governments, are as much within the design and care of the Constitution as the preservation of the Union and the maintenance of the National government.' The necessity of preserving each from every form of illegitimate intrusion or interference on the part of the other is so imperative as to require this court, when its judicial power is properly invoked, to view with a careful and discriminating eye any legislation challenged as constituting such an intrusion or interference. See South Carolina v. United States, 199 U.S. 437, 448, 26 S.Ct. 110, 50 L.Ed. 261, 4 Ann.Cas. 737.

The precise question, therefore, which we are required to answer by an application of these principles is whether the congressional act contemplates a surrender by the state to the federal government, in whole or in part, of any state governmental power to administer its own unemployment law or the state pay roll-tax funds which it has collected for the purposes of that law. An affirmative answer to this question, I think, must be made.

I do not, of course, doubt the power of the state to select and utilize a depository for the safe-keeping of its funds; but it is quite another thing to agree with the selected depository that the funds shall be withdrawn for certain stipulated purposes, and for no other. Nor do I doubt the authority of the federal government and a state government to co-operate to a common end, provided each of them is authorized to reach it. But such co-operation must be effectuated by an exercise of the powers which they severally possess, and not by an exercise, through invasion or surrender, by one of them of the governmental power of the other.

An illustration of what I regard as permissible co-operation is to be found in title I of the act now under consideration. By that title, federal appropriations for old age assistance are authorized to be made to any state which shall have adopted a plan for old-age assistance conforming to designated requirements. But the state is not obliged, as a condition of having the federal bounty, to deposit in the federal treasury funds raised by the state. The state keeps its own funds and administers its own law in respect of them, without let or hindrance of any kind on the part of the federal government; so that we have simply the familiar case of federal aid upon conditions which the state, without surrendering any of its powers, may accept or not as it chooses. Massachusetts v. Mellon, 262 U.S. 447, 480, 482, 483, 43 S. Ct. 597, 598, 599, 67 L.Ed. 1078.

But this is not the situation with which we are called upon to deal in the present case. For here, the state must deposit the proceeds of its taxation in the federal treasury, upon terms which make the deposit suspiciously like a forced loan to be repaid only in accordance with restrictions imposed by federal law. Title IX, §§ 903(a)(3), 904(a), (b), (e), 42 U.S.C.A. §§ 1103(a) (3), 1104(a, b, e). All moneys withdrawn from this fund must be used exclusively for the payment of compensation. Section 903(a)(4), 42 U.S.C.A. § 1103(a)(4). And this compensation is to be paid through public employment offices in the state or such other agencies as a federal board may approve. Section 903(a)(1), 42 U.S.C.A. § 1103(a)(1). The act, it is true, recognizes section 903(a)(6), 42 U.S.C.A. § 1103(a)(6) the power of the Legislature to amend or repeal its compensation law at any time. But there is nothing in the act, as I read it, which justifies the conclusion that the state may, in that event, unconditionally withdraw its funds from the federal treasury. Section 903(b), 42 U.S.C.A. § 1103(b), provides that the board shall certify in each taxable year to the Secretary of the Treasury each state whose law has been approved. But the board is forbidden to certify any state which the board finds has so changed its law that it no longer contains the provisions specified in subsection (a), 'or has with respect to such taxable year failed to comply substantially with any such provision.' The federal government, therefore, in the person of its agent, the board, sits not only as a perpetual overseer, interpreter and censor of state legislation on the subject, but, as lord paramount, to determine whether the state is faithfully executing its own law—as though the state were a dependency under pupilage 1 and not to be trusted. The foregoing, taken in connection with the provisions that money withdrawn can be used only in payment of compensation and that it must be paid through an agency approved by the federal board, leaves it, to say the least, highly uncertain whether the right of the state to withdraw any part of its own funds exists, under the act, otherwise than upon these various statutory conditions. It is true also that subsection (f) of section 904, 42 U.S.C.A. § 1104(f), authorizes the Secretary of the Treasury to pay to any state agency 'such amount as it may duly requisition, not exceeding the amount standing to the account of such State agency at the time of such payment.' But it is to be observed that the payment is to be made to the state agency, and only such amount as that agency may duly requisition. It is hard to find in this provision any extension of the right of the state to withdraw its funds except in the manner and for the specific purpose prescribed by the act.

By these various provisions of the act, the federal agencies are authorized to supervise and hamper the administrative powers of the state to a degree which not only does not comport with the dignity of a quasi sovereign state—a matter with which we are not judicially concerned but which deny to it that supremacy and freedom from external interference in respect of its affairs which the Constitution contemplates—a matter of very definite judicial concern. I refer to some, though by no means all, of the cases in point.

In the License Cases, 5 How. 504, 588, 12 L.Ed. 256, Mr. Justice McLean said that the federal government was supreme within the scope of its delegated powers, and the state governments equally supreme in the exercise of the powers not delegated nor inhibited to them; that the states exercise their powers over everything connected with their social and internal condition; and that over these subjects the federal government had no power. 'They appertain to the State sovereignty as exclusively as powers exclusively delegated appertain to the general government.'

In Tarble's Case, 13 Wall. 397, 20 L.Ed. 597, Mr. Justice Field, after pointing out that the general government and the state are separate and distinct sovereignties, acting separately and independently of each other within their respective spheres, said that, except in one particular, they stood in the same independent relation to each other as they would if their authority embraced distinct territories. The one particular referred to is that of the supremacy of the authority of the United States in case of conflict between the two.

In Farrington v. Tennessee, 95 U.S. 679, 685, 24 L.Ed. 558, this court said, 'Yet every State has a sphere of action where the authority of the national government may not intrude. Within that domain the State is as if the union were not. Such are the checks and balances in our complicated but wise system of State and national polity.'

'The powers exclusively given to the federal government,' it was said in Worcester v. State of Georgia, 6 Pet. 515, 570, 8 L.Ed. 483, 'are limitations upon the state authorities. But with the exception of these limitations, the states are supreme; and their sovereignty can be no more invaded by the action of the general government, than the action of the state governments can arrest or obstruct the course of the national power.'

The force of what has been said is not broken by an acceptance of the view that the state is not coerced by the federal law. The effect of the dual distribution of powers is completely to deny to the states whatever is granted exclusively to the nation, and, conversely, to deny to the nation whatever is reserved exclusively to the states. 'The determination of the Framers Convention and the ratifying conventions to preserve complete and unimpaired state self government in all matters not committed to the general government is one of the plainest facts which emerges from the history of their deliberations. And adherence to that determination is incumbent equally upon the federal government and the states. State powers can neither be appropriated on the one hand nor abdicated on the other.' Carter v. Carter Coal Co., supra, 298 U.S. 238, at page 295, 56 S.Ct. 855, 866, 80 L.Ed. 1160. The purpose of the Constitution in that regard does not admit of doubt or qualification; and it can be thwarted no more by voluntary surrender from within than by invasion from without.

Nor may the constitutional objection suggested be overcome by the expectation of public benefit resulting from the federal participation authorized by the act. Such expectation, if voiced in support of a proposed constitutional enactment, would be quite proper for the consideration of the legislative body. But, as we said in the Carter Case, supra, 298 U.S. 238, at page 291, 56 S.Ct.

855, 864, 80 L.Ed. 1160, 'nothing is more certain than that beneficent aims, however great or well directed, can never serve in lieu of constitutional power.' Moreover, everything which the act seeks to do for the relief of unemployment might have been accomplished, as is done by this same act for the relief of the misfortunes of old age, without obliging the state to surrender, or share with another government, any of its powers.

If we are to survive as the United States, the balance between the powers of the nation and those of the states must be maintained. There is grave danger in permitting it to dip in either direction, danger—if there were no other—in the precedent thereby set for further departures from the equipoise. The threat implicit in the present encroachment upon the administrative functions of the states is that greater encroachments, and encroachments upon other functions, will follow.

For the foregoing reasons, I think the judgment below should be reversed.

Mr. Justice VAN DEVANTER joins in this opinion.
Mr. Justice BUTLER, dissenting.

I think that the objections to the challenged enactment expressed in the separate opinions of Mr. Justice McREYNOLDS and Mr. Justice SUTHERLAND are well taken. I am also of opinion that, in principle and as applied to bring about and to gain control over state unemployment compensation, the statutory scheme is repugnant to the Tenth Amendment: 'The powers not delegated to the United States by the Constitution, nor prohibited by it to the States, are reserved to the States respectively, or to the people.' The Constitution grants to the United States no power to pay unemployed persons or to require the states to enact laws or to raise or disburse money for that purpose. The provisions in question, if not amounting to coercion in a legal sense, are manifestly designed and intended directly to affect state action in the respects specified. And, if valid as so employed, this 'tax and credit' device may be made effective to enable federal authorities to induce, if not indeed to compel, state enactments for any purpose within the realm of state power and generally to control state administration of state laws.

The act creates a Social Security Board and imposes upon it the duty of studying and making recommendations as to legislation and as to administrative policies concerning unemployment compensation and related subjects. Section 702, 42 U.S.C.A. § 902. It authorizes grants of money by the United States to States for old age assistance, for administration of unemployment compensation, for aid to dependent children, for maternal and child welfare and for public health. Each grant depends upon state compliance with conditions prescribed by federal authority. The amounts given being within the discretion of the Congress, it may at any time make available federal money sufficient effectively to influence state policy, standards and details of administration.

The excise laid by section 901 (42 U.S.C.A. § 1101) is limited to specified employers. It is not imposed to raise money to pay unemployment compensation. But it is imposed having regard to that subject for, upon enactment of state laws for that purpose in conformity with federal requirements specified in the act, each of the employers subject to the federal tax becomes entitled to credit for the amount he pays into an unemployment fund under a state law up to 90 per cent. of the federal tax. The amounts yielded by the remaining 10 per cent., not assigned to any specific purpose, may be applied to pay the federal contributions and expenses in respect of state unemployment compensation. It is not yet possible to determine more closely the sums that will be needed for these purposes.

When the federal act was passed, Wisconsin was the only state paying unemployment compensation. Though her plan then in force is by students of the subject generally deemed the best yet devised, she found it necessary to change her law in order to secure federal approval. In the absence of that, Wisconsin employers subject to the federal tax would not have been allowed Sec. 903. (a) The Social Security Board shall approve any State law submitted to it, within thirty days of such submission, which it finds provides that— (1) All compensation is to be paid through public employment offices in the State or such other agencies as the Board may approve; (2) No compensation shall be payable with respect to any day of unemployment occurring within two years after the first day of the first period with respect to which contributions are required; (3) All money received in the unemployment fund shall immediately upon such receipt be paid over to the Secretary of the Treasury to the credit of the Unemployment Trust Fund established by Section 904 (section 1104 of this any deduction on account of their contribution to the state fund. Any state would be moved to conform to federal requirements, not utterly objectionable, in order to save its taxpayers from the federal tax imposed in addition to the contributions under state laws.

Federal agencies prepared and took draft bills to state Legislatures to enable and induce them to pass laws providing for unemployment compensation in accordance with federal requirements and thus to obtain relief for the employers from the impending federal exaction. Obviously the act creates the peril of federal tax not to raise revenue but to persuade. Of course, each state was free to reject any measure so proposed. But, if it failed to adopt a plan acceptable to federal authority, the full burden of the federal tax would be exacted. And, as federal demands similarly conditioned may be increased from time to time as Congress shall determine, possible federal pressure in that field is without limit. Already at least forty-three states, yielding to the inducement resulting immediately from the application of the federal tax and credit device, have provided for unemployment compensation in form to merit approval of the Social Security

Board. Presumably the remaining States will comply whenever convenient for their Legislatures to pass the necessary laws. The terms of the measure make it clear that the tax and credit device was intended to enable federal officers virtually to control the exertion of powers of the states in a field in which they alone have jurisdiction and from which the United States is by the Constitution excluded.

I am of opinion that the judgment of the Circuit Court of Appeals should be reversed.

SUPREME COURT OF THE UNITED STATES

NO. 910.--OCTOBER Term 1936

Guy T. Helvering, Commissioner of Internal Revenue, and
William M. Welch, Collector of Internal Revenue for the District
of Massachusetts, The Edison Electric Illuminating Company of
Boston, Petitioners,

vs.

George P. Davis, Respondent.

On Writ of Certiorari to the United States Circuit Court of
Appeals for the First Circuit.

[May 24, 1937.]

Mr. Justice Cardozo delivered the opinion of the Court.

The Social Security Act (Act of August 14, 1935, c. 531, 49 Stat
620, 42 U. S. C., c. 7, (Supp.)) is challenged once again.

In No. 837, *Steward Machine Co. v. Davis,--U.S.--,* decided this
day, we have upheld the validity of Title IX of the act, imposing an
excise upon employers of eight or more. In this case Titles VIII and
II are the subject of attack. Title VIII lays another excise upon
employers in addition to the one imposed by Title IX (though with
different exemptions). It lays a special income tax upon
employees to be deducted from their wages and paid by the
employers. Title II provides for the payment of Old Age Benefits,
and supplies the motive and occasion, in the view of the assailants
of the statute, for the levy of the taxes imposed by Title VIII. The
plan of the two titles will now be summarized more fully.

Title VIII, as we have said, lays two different types of tax, an
"income tax on employees", and "an excise tax on employers."
The income tax on employees is measured by wages paid during

the calendar year. Section 801. The excise tax on the employer is to be paid "with respect to having individuals in his employ", and, like the tax on employees, is measured by wages. Section 804. Neither tax is applicable to certain types of employment, such as agricultural labor, domestic service, service for the national or state governments, and service performed by persons who have attained the age of 65 years. Section 811 (b). The two taxes are at the same rate. Sections 801, 804. For the years 1937 to 1939, inclusive, the rate for each tax is fixed at one per cent. Thereafter the rate increases of 1 per cent every three years, until after December 31, 1948, the rate for each tax reaches 3 per cent. *Ibid.* In the computation of wages all remuneration is to be included except so much as is in excess of $3,000 during the calendar year affected. Section 811 (a). The income tax on employees is to be collected by the employer, who is to deduct the amount from the wages "as and when paid". Section 802 (a). He is indemnified against claims and demands of any person by reason of such payment. *Ibid.* The proceeds of both taxes are to be paid into the Treasury like internal-revenue taxes generally, and are not earmarked in any way. Section 807 (a). There are penalties for nonpayment. Section 807 (c).

Title II has the caption "Federal Old-Age Benefits." The benefits are of two types, first, monthly pensions, and second, lump sum payments, the payments of the second class being relatively few and unimportant.

The first section of this title creates an account in the United States Treasury to be known as the "Old-Age Reserve Account". Section 201. No present appropriation, however, is made to that account. All that the statute does is to authorize appropriations annually thereafter, beginning with the fiscal year which ends June 30, 1937. How large they shall be is not known in advance.

The "amount sufficient as an annual premium" to provide for the required payments is "to be determined on a reserve basis in accordance with accepted actuarial principles, and based upon such tables of mortality as the Secretary of the Treasury shall from time to time adopt, and upon an interest rate of 3 per centum per annum compounded annually." Section 201 (a). Not a dollar goes into the Account by force of the challenged act alone, unaided by acts to follow.

Section 202 and later sections prescribe the form of benefits. The principal type is a monthly pension payable to a person after he as attained the age of 65. This benefit is available only to one who has worked for at least one day in each of at least five separate years since December 31, 1936, who has earned at least $2,000 since that date, and who is not then receiving wages "with respect to regular employment." Sections 202 (a), (d), 210 (c). The benefits are not to begin before January 1, 1942. Section 202 (a). In no event are they to exceed $85 a month. Section 202 (b). They are to be measured (subject to that limit) by a percentage of the wages the percentage decreasing at stated intervals as the wages become higher. Section 202 (a). In addition to the monthly benefits, provision is made in certain contingencies for "lump sum payments" of secondary importance. A summary by the Government of the four situations calling for such payments is printed in the margin.[1]

This suit is brought by a shareholder of the Edison Electric Illuminating Company of Boston, a Massachusetts corporation, to restrain the corporation from making the payments and deductions called for by the act, which is stated to be void under the Constitution of the United States. The bill tells us that the corporation has decided to obey the statute, that it has reached this decision in the face of the complainant's protests, and that it will make the payments and deductions unless restrained by a decree. The expected consequences are indicated substantially as follows: The deductions from the wages of the employees will produce unrest among them, and will be followed, it is predicted, by demands that wages be increased. If the exactions shall ultimately be held void, the company will have parted with moneys which as a practical matter it will be impossible to recover. Nothing is said in the bill about the promise of indemnity. The prediction is made also that serious consequences will ensue if there is a submission to the excise. The corporation and its shareholders will suffer irreparable loss, and many thousands of dollars will be subtracted from the value of the shares. The prayer is for an injunction and for a declaration that the act is void.

The corporation appeared and answered without raising any issue of fact. Later the United States Commissioner of Internal Revenue and the United States Collector for the District of Massachusetts, petitioners in this court, were allowed to intervene. They moved to strike so much of the bill as has relation to the tax on employees taking the ground that the employer not being subject to tax under those provisions, may not challenge their validity, and that the complainant shareholder, whose rights are no greater than those of his corporation, has even less standing to be heard on such a question. The intervening defendants also filed an answer which restated the point raised in the motion to strike, and maintained the validity of Title VIII in all its parts. The District Court held that the tax upon employees was not properly at issue, and that the tax upon employers was constitutional. It thereupon denied the prayer for an injunction, and dismissed the bill. On appeal to the Circuit Court of Appeals for the First Circuit, the decree was reversed, one judge dissenting. --F. (2d) --. The court held that Title II was void as an invasion of powers reserved by the Tenth Amendment to the states or to the people and that Title II in collapsing carried Title VIII along with it. As an additional reason for invalidating the tax upon employers, the court held that it was not an excise as excises were understood when the Constitution was adopted. Cf. *Davis v. Boston & Maine R. R. Co.,*--F. (2d)--, decided the same day.

A petition for certiorari followed. It was filed by the intervening defendants, the Commissioner and the Collector, and brought two questions, and two only, to our notice. We were asked to determine: (1) "whether the tax imposed upon employers by Section 804 of the Social Security Act is within the power of

Congress under tile Constitution", and (2) "whether the validity of the tax imposed upon employees by Section 801 of the Social Security Act is properly in issue in this case, and if it is, whether that tax is within the power of Congress under the Constitution." The defendant corporation gave notice to the Clerk that it joined in the petition, but it has taken no part in any subsequent proceedings. A writ of certiorari issued.

First: Questions as to the remedy invoked by the complainant confront us at the outset.

Was the conduct of the company in resolving to pay the taxes a legitimate exercise of the discretion of the directors? Has petitioner a standing to challenge that resolve in the absence of an adequate showing of irreparable injury? Does the acquiescence of the company in the equitable remedy affect the answer to those questions? Though power may still be ours to take such objections for ourselves, is acquiescence effective to rid us of the duty? Is duty modified still further by the attitude of the Government, its waiver of a defense under section 3224 of the Revised Statutes, its waiver of a defense that the legal remedy is adequate, its earnest request that we determine whether the law shall stand or fall? The writer of this opinion believes that the remedy is ill conceived, that in a controversy such as this a court must refuse to give equitable relief when a cause of action in equity is neither pleaded nor proved, and that the suit for an injunction should be dismissed upon that ground. He thinks this course should be followed in adherence to the general rule that constitutional questions are not to be determined in the absence of strict necessity. In that view he is supported by Mr. Justice BRANDEIS Mr. Justice STONE and Mr. Justice ROBERTS. However, a majority of the court have reached a different conclusion they find in this case extraordinary features making it fitting in their judgment to determine whether the benefits and the taxes are valid or invalid. They distinguish *Norman v. Consolidated Gas Co.,-* -F. (2d) --, recently decided by the Court of Appeals for the Second Circuit, on the ground that in that case, the remedy was

124

challenged by the company and the Government at every stage of the proceeding, thus withdrawing from the court any marginal discretion. The ruling of the majority removes from the case the preliminary objection as to the nature of the remedy which we took of our own motion at the beginning of the argument. Under the compulsion of that ruling, the merits are now here.

Second: The scheme of benefits created by the provisions of Title II is not in contravention of the limitations of the Tenth Amendment.

Congress may spend money in aid of the "general welfare". Constitution, Art. I, section 8; *United States v. Butler,* 297 U. S. *1, 65; Steward Machine Co. v. Davis, supra.* There have been great statesmen in our history who have stood for other views. We will not resurrect the contest. It is now settled by decision. *United States v. Butler, supra* The conception of the spending power advocated by Hamilton and strongly reinforced by Story has prevailed over that of Madison, which has not been lacking in adherents. Yet difficulties are left when the power is conceded. The line must still be drawn between one welfare and another, between particular and general. Where this shall be placed cannot be known through a formula in advance of the event. There is a middle ground or certainly a penumbra in which discretion is at large. The discretion, however, is not confided to the courts. The discretion belongs to Congress, unless the choice is clearly wrong, a display of arbitrary power is not an exercise of judgment. This is now familiar law. "When such a contention comes here we naturally require a showing that by no reasonable possibility can the challenged legislation fall within the wide range of discretion permitted to the Congress." *United States v. Butler, supra, p.* 67 Cf. *Cincinnati Soap Co. v United States, May 3, 1937,-- U. S.; United States v. Realty Co.* 163 U. S. 427, 440; *Head Money Cases,* 112 U. S. 580, 595. Nor is the concept of the general welfare static. Needs that were narrow or parochial a century ago may be interwoven in our day with the well-being of the nation. What is critical or urgent changes with the times.

The purge of nation-wide calamity that began in 1929 has taught us many lessons. Not the least is the solidarity of interests that may once have seemed to be divided. Unemployment spreads from state to state, the hinterland now settled that in pioneer days gave an avenue of escape. *Home Building & Loan Association v. Blaisdell,* 290 U. S. 398, 442. Spreading from state to state, unemployment is an ill not particular but general, which may be checked, if Congress so determines, by the resources of the nation. If this can have been doubtful until now, our ruling today in the case of the *Steward Machine Co. supra,* has set the doubt at rest. But the ill is all one or at least not greatly different whether men are thrown out of work because there is no longer work to do or because the disabilities of age make them incapable of doing it. Rescue becomes necessary irrespective of the cause. The hope behind this statute is to save men and women from the rigors of the poor house as well as from the haunting fear that such a lot awaits them when journey's end is near.

Congress did not improvise a judgment when it found that the award of old age benefits would be conducive to the general welfare The President's Committee on Economic Security made an investigation and report, aided by a research staff of Government officers and employees, and by an Advisory Council and seven other advisory groups.[2] Extensive hearings followed before the House Committee on Ways and Means and the Senate Committee on Finance.[3] A great mass of evidence was brought together supporting the policy which finds expression in the act. Among the relevant facts are these: The number of persons in the United States 65 years of age or over is increasing proportionately as well as absolutely. What is even more important the number of such persons unable to take care of themselves is growing at a threatening pace. More and more our population is becoming urban and industrial instead of rural and agricultural.[4] The evidence is impressive that among industrial workers the younger men and women are preferred over the older.[5] In time of retrenchment the older are commonly the first to go, and even if retained, their wages are likely to be lowered. The plight of men and women at so low an age as 40 is hard, almost hopeless, when they are driven to seek for reemployment. Statistics are in the brief. A few illustrations will be chosen from many there collected. In 1930, out of 224 American factories investigated, 71, or almost one third, had fixed maximum hiring age limits; in 4 plants the limit was under 40; in 41 it was under 46. In the other 153 plants there were no fixed limits, but in practice few were hired if they were over 50 years of age.[6] With the loss of savings inevitable in periods of idleness, the fate of workers over 65, when thrown out of work, is little less than desperate. A recent study of the Social Security Board informs us that "one-fifth of the aged in the United States were receiving old age assistance, emergency relief, institutional care, employment under the works program, or some other form of aid from public or private funds; two-fifths to one-half were dependent on friends and relatives, one-eighth had some income from earnings; and possibly one-sixth had some savings or property. Approximately three out of four persons 65 or over were probably dependent wholly or partially on others for support."[7] We summarize in the margin the results of other studies by state and national commissions.[8] They point the same way.

The problem is plainly national in area and dimensions. Moreover laws of the separate states cannot deal with it effectively. Congress, at least, had a basis for that belief. States and local governments are often lacking in the resources that are necessary to finance an adequate program of security for the aged. This is brought out with a wealth of illustration in recent studies of the problem.[9] Apart from the failure of resources, states and local governments are at times reluctant to increase so heavily the burden of taxation to be borne by their residents for fear of placing themselves in a position of economic disadvantage as compared with neighbors or competitors. We have seen this in our study of the problem of unemployment compensation. *Steward Machine Co. v. Davis, supra.* A system of old age pensions has special dangers of its own, if put in force in one state and rejected in another. The existence of such a system is a bait to the needy and dependent elsewhere, encouraging them to migrate and seek a haven of repose. Only a power that is national call serve the interests of all.

Whether wisdom or unwisdom resides in the scheme of benefits set forth in Title II, it is not for us to say. The answer to such inquiries must come from Congress, not the courts. Our concern here as often is with power, not with wisdom. Counsel for respondent has recalled to us the virtues of self-reliance and frugality. There is a possibility, he says, that aid from a paternal government may sap those sturdy virtues and breed a race of weaklings. If Massachusetts so believes and shapes her laws in that conviction must her breed of sons be changed, he asks, because some other philosophy of government finds favor in the halls of Congress? But the answer is not doubtful. One might ask with equal reason whether the system of protective tariffs is to be set aside at will in one state or another whenever local policy prefers the rule of *laissez faire.* The issue is a closed one. It was fought out long ago.[10] When money is spent to promote the general welfare, the concept of welfare or the opposite is shaped by Congress, not the states. So the concept be not arbitrary, the locality must yield. Constitution, Art VI, Par. 2.

Third: Title II being valid, there is no occasion to inquire whether Title VIII would have to fall if Title II were set at naught.

The argument for the respondent is that the provisions of the two titles dovetail in such a way as to justify the conclusion that Congress would have been unwilling to pass one without the other. The argument for petitioners is that the tax moneys are not earmarked, and that Congress is at liberty to spend them as it will. The usual separability clause is embodied in the act. Section 1103.

We find it unnecessary to make a choice between the arguments and so leave the question open.

Fourth: The tax upon employers is a valid excise or duty upon the relation of employment.

As to this we need not add to our opinion in *Steward Machine vs. Davis, supra,* where we considered a like question in respect of Title IX.

Fifth: The tax is not invalid as a result of its exemptions.

Here again the opinion in *Steward Machine Co. v. Davis supra* says all that need be said.

Sixth: The decree of the Court of Appeals should be reversed and that of the District Court affirmed.

Ordered accordingly.

Mr. Justice McREYNOLDS and Mr. Justice BUTLER are of opinion that the provisions of the Act here challenged are repugnant to the Tenth Amendment, and that the decree of the Circuit Court of Appeals should be affirmed.

NOTICE: Please pause here and revisit the term *parens.patriae*. Regardless of our ignorance as a people, did you ever think the federal government would refer to you as a child or as incompetent? Are free people actually *free* under such pretense? The mere presence of Americans within the jurisdiction of the United States may be a matter of how the government views us and how we no longer account for ourselves. This observation is offered because of the chapter you are about to read. As you proceed, ask yourself why you grant judges such instant and pervasive credibility. Who are these black-robed men and women but those who are enticed by power, if only subtly applied, and without the discipline to tack along a narrow thread of thought concerning the constitutional limits of government?

Cardozo's Perspective

58)   Supreme Court Justice Cardozo wrote the opinions for Steward Machine and Helvering. It may be stated rather easily that he strained to justify a judicial opinion which defied the history of America since its founding. As stated in his opinion is Steward Machine, he rationalized that,

> In 1777, before our Constitutional Convention, **Parliament laid upon employers** an annual 'duty' of 21 shillings for **'every male Servant' employed** in stated forms of work.3 Revenue Act of 1777, 17 George III, c. 39.4 The point is made as a distinction that tax upon **the use of male servants was thought of as a tax upon a luxury**. Davis v. Boston & Maine R.R. Co., supra. **It did not touch employments in husbandry or business. This is to throw over the argument that historically an excise is a tax upon the enjoyment of commodities.** But the attempted distinction, whatever may be thought of its validity, is inapplicable to a statute of Virginia passed in 1780. There a tax of 3 pounds, 6 shillings, and 8 pence was to be paid for every male tithable above the age of twenty-one years (with stated exceptions), and a like tax for 'every white servant whatsoever, except apprentices under the age of twenty one years.' 10 Hening's Statutes of Virginia, p. 244. **Our colonial forbears knew more about ways of taxing than some of their descendants seem to be willing to concede.**

59)   Given Cardozo's effort to justify a tax that was historically unprecedented, we must acknowledge his judicial philosophy to understand his motives. In his book, The Nature of the Judicial Process,[21] he states,

---

[21] http://www.constitution.org/cmt/cardozo/jud_proc.htm

I take judge made law as one of the existing realities of life. (p. 2)

60) Since Cardozo believes in "judge made law," we may appreciate how the concept of the "relation of employment" prevailed. We may appreciate how and why the Social Security Act *endured* a court challenge. Consider his perspective on precedent—that is deciding cases based upon the preceding understanding of the law with respect to prior cases.

> But, of course, **no system of living law can be evolved by such a process**, and no judge of a high court, worthy of his office, views the function of his place so narrowly. If that were all there was to our calling, there would be little of intellectual interest about it. (p. 8)

Not only does he view the law as "living," he discounts precedent on a wholesale basis and excuses the Court's deviation from timeless truths, truths which are now malleable with a law that lives or morphs into what was never conceivable.

61) Cardozo believed there were four main factors by which a judge makes a decision: philosophy, history, tradition, and social welfare. When discussing the role of history, he reveals an element of his thinking which should give us pause. He states that when making a decision,

> A residuum will be left where the **personality of the judge, his taste, his training his bent of mind**, may prove the controlling factor. (p. 30)

62) Cardozo compares philosophy with history.

Sometimes the prevailing tendencies exhibited in the current writings of philosophical jurists may sway the balance. There are **vogues and fashions in jurisprudence** as in **literature and art and dress**. (p. 33)

63)   When custom or tradition enters the formula of judicial decision making, he opines,

> The triers of the facts in determining whether that standard has been attained must **consult the habits of life, the everyday beliefs and practices**, of the men and women about them. Innumerable, also, are the cases where the course of dealing to be followed is defined by customs, or, more properly speaking, the usages, of a particular trade or market or profession. The constant assumption runs throughout the law that natural and spontaneous evolutions of habit fix the limits of right and wrong. (p. 37)

64)   Cardozo finishes his discussion of philosophy, history, and custom stating they "have their place." He then offers,

> **We will shape the law to conform to them when we may; but, only within bounds**. The end which the law serves will dominate them all. (p. 39)

65)   What is that "end" which will dominate? According to Cardozo, it is "social justice."

> From history and philosophy and custom, we pass, therefore, to **the force which in our day and generation is becoming the greatest of them all, the power of social justice**. (p. 38)

Cardozo posits,

> Finally, when the social needs demand one settlement
> rather than another, there are times when we **must bend
> symmetry, ignore history and sacrifice custom** in the
> pursuit of larger ends. (P. 38)

66) We have a sense of the "larger ends" when he states judges

> ... are called upon to say how far existing rules are to be
> extended or restricted, they must **let the welfare of
> society fix the path, its direction and distance**. (p. 39)

67) What does Cardozo mean by "social welfare?"

> **Social welfare** is a broad term. I use it to cover many
> concepts more or less allied. It may mean what is commonly
> spoken of as public policy, **the good of the collective body**.
> (p. 43)

68) Cardozo stresses the importance of social welfare.

> It is true, I think, today in every department of the law that
> **the social value of a rule** has become a test of growing
> power and importance. (p. 43)

69) Cardozo bluntly states,

> The final **cause of law is the welfare of society.** (p. 39)

70) Cardozo explains his perspective as to the role of the court.

In every case, without exception, it is the business of the court to supply what the state omits, but always by means of an interpretive function. (p. 42)

71)   For Cardozo, the interpretive function is closely associated with what he referred to as a

...**new political philosophy**...reflected in the work of statesmen and ultimately in the decrees of the courts. (p. 47)

72)   With a penchant for citing foreign legal thought and international sentiment, Cardozo referred to Dicey in <u>Law and Opinion in England</u> for this "new political philosophy."

"The movement from individualistic liberalism to **unsystematic collectivism**" had **brought changes in the social order** which carried with them **the need of a new formulation of fundamental rights and duties**. (p. 47)

73)   Cardozo cites that America was slow to assert this mindset, but that

a new conception of the significance of constitutional limitations in the domain of individual liberty, emerged to recognition and dominance. (p. 47)

Those who sense Cardozo's judicial philosophy and objectives should be troubled with his beliefs and approach. He did not write of individual or natural rights or the sanctity of the Constitution and its inherent constraints upon the federal government. Rather, we read the opposite. Note how Cardozo viewed the courts.

Courts know today that statutes are to be viewed, not in isolation or in vacuo, as pronouncements of abstract principles for the guidance of an ideal community, but in **the setting and framework of present day conditions, as revealed by the labors of economists and students of the social sciences in our country and abroad**. (p. 49)

74) It would be appropriate to question whether or not a man's labor and earnings, his property, would be second to the social welfare aims of an activist Supreme Court. If the foregoing is not unsettling, consider Cardozo's next thought.

The same fluid and dynamic conception which underlies the modern notion of liberty, as secured to the individual by the constitutional immunity must also underlie the cognate notion of equality. No state shall deny to any person within its jurisdiction "the equal protection of the laws." Restrictions, viewed narrowly, may seem to foster inequality. The same restrictions, when viewed broadly, may be seen "to be necessary in the long run in order to establish the equality of position between the parties in which the liberality of contract begins." (p. 50)

75) Cardozo's conclusion is inconsistent with basic American principles of limited constitutional government.

From all this, it results that the content of **constitutional immunities is not constant but varies from age to age**. (p. 50)

76) Cardozo failed to respect the limits of the Constitution and the truth it represents. As if in overdrive, he, once again, refers to foreign jurists.

> I think it is interesting to note that even in the interpretation of ordinary statutes, there are jurists, at any rate abroad, who maintain that **the meaning today is not always the meaning of tomorrow**. (p. 51)

77) Cardozo cites the highest official of the French courts.

> "We do not inquire what the legislator willed a century ago, but what he would have willed had he known what our present conditions would be." (p. 51)

78) Cardozo clearly moved beyond the concrete virtues of the Constitution. Consider his comments about property, which conflict with a perspective that many believe to be sacrosanct.

> **Property, like liberty**, though immune under the Constitution from destruction, **is not immune from regulation essential for the common good**. What that regulation shall be, **every generation must work out for itself.** (p. 53)

79) This sentiment leads to a defining position. Cardozo said,

> The courts, then, are free in making the limits of the individual's immunities to shape their judgments in accordance with reason and justice. (p. 54)

80) Cardozo does not believe a judge should rely upon his own "reason and justice."

> It is what I reasonably believe some other man of normal intellect and conscience might reasonably look upon as right. (p. 54)

81) Is Cardozo's judicial posture sound, noble, or practical? How does he gauge what is normal? Are the justices who strongly dissented in Steward Machine and Helvering normal? Is the man who cherishes a strict constructionist interpretation of the Constitution concerning his property normal? Is the man who aspires for self-sufficiency with his natural God-given rights the measure of normal? Those who would respond affirmatively to the last two questions would not readily embrace what is *right* according to Cardozo's progressive normal.

82) The essential question concerns the passing of 150 years of prevailing thought with a philosophy, history, custom, and social justice whereby man provides for himself and extends charity to his fellow man without the dictates of a federal government, the shackles of a supposed federal power known as the doctrine of **parens patriae** or a self-promoting high Court. The question of "property" was the cornerstone of man's existence—his very being. The greatest public use of property was anchored in private application. The bounty of a man's life was not measured by his security or material wealth, but his ability to live in freedom. The Constitution was the means to ensure the legislative, executive and judicial branches of government could not and would not adversely alter what was not within its jurisdiction.

83) Cardozo's perspective of the Constitution reveals much.

I speak first of the constitution, and in particular of the great immunities with which it surrounds the individual. No one shall be deprived of liberty without due process of law. Here is a concept of greatest generality. Yet it is put before the courts en bloc. **Liberty is not defined. Its limits are not mapped and charted. How shall they be known? Does liberty mean the same thing for successive generations? May restraints that are arbitrary yesterday be useful and rational and therefore lawful today? May constraints that are arbitrary today become useful and rational and therefore lawful tomorrow? I have no doubt that the answer to these questions must be yes.** There were times in our judicial history when the answer might have been no. **Liberty was conceived of at first as something static and absolute.** The Declaration of Independence had enshrined it. The political philosophy of Rousseau and of Locke and later of Herbert Spencer and the Manchester school of economics had dignified and rationalized it. Laissez faire was not only a counsel of caution which statesmen would do well to heed. It was a categorical imperative which statesmen, as well as judges, must obey. The "nineteenth century theory" was "one of the eternal conceptions involved in the idea of justice and containing potentially an exact rule for every case to be reached by an absolute process of logical deduction." **The century had not closed, however, before a new political philosophy became reflected in the work of statesmen and ultimately of the courts.** (p. 46-47)

84)   Cardozo was a jurist who "evolved" and was malleable with the times. The principles which forged America were secondary to an interpretation of another man of "normal intellect and conscience." It was Cardozo's view of the future, not the tried-

and-true credentials of the past, which led to his notion of "social justice." His "living law" was an antidote which failed. His opinion in <u>Steward Machine</u> was a death knell to a spirit of perseverance which has resulted in a state of dependency in America. Just as grave a consequence, Cardozo contributed to a belief that this country was a "common mass," which countered the wisdom of past justices, those who exercised restraint for a country where independence was cherished.

Jurisdiction

85)   As a practical matter, we now know how Americans enter the jurisdiction of the *United States*. Since an excise tax is upon a voluntary act, upon the acceptance of a federal privilege, the government gains jurisdiction. Yet, Congress, by simply declaring the nature of employment and the availability of Social Security, did not effectively alter how people thought and lived. Congress did not expand the jurisdiction of the *United States*. If Congress exercised a legitimate power to tax, it was a power it had already. The main question is who becomes liable for the tax and why?

86)   People who did not enter the relation of employment or voluntarily accept the federal privilege of Social Security were unaffected. The government could not force people to accept a benefit. Non participants—non taxpayers—remained without the United States for the purpose of the income tax. To understand the scheme, we must appreciate the concept of jurisdiction. For, without jurisdiction the government has nothing.

> Ju-ris-dic-tion (noun) 1) the power, right or authority to interpret and apply a law, 2) the authority of a sovereign power, 3) the limits or territory within which authority may be exercised. *Merriam Webster's Dictionary and Thesaurus, 2007*

87)   The United States has jurisdiction through and by 18 powers delegated to it under Article 1, Section 8 of the Constitution. The *United States* has exclusive jurisdiction over territory it controls.

> The Congress shall have Power To exercise **exclusive Legislation in all Cases whatsoever, over such District** (not

exceeding ten Miles square) as may, by Cession of particular States, and the acceptance of Congress, become the Seat of Government of the United States, and to exercise like Authority over all Places purchased by the Consent of the Legislature of the State in which the Same shall be, for the Erection of Forts, Magazines, Arsenals, dock-yards and other needful buildings. *United States Constitution, Article 1, Section 8, Clause 17*

88) The Supreme Court considered the question of jurisdiction.

The exclusive jurisdiction which the United States have in forts and dock-yards ceded to them, is derived from the express assent of the states by whom the cessions are made. It could be derived in no other manner; because without it, the authority of the state would be supreme and exclusive therein. *United States v Bevans*, *3 Wheat 336,* 350-351 (1818)

89) In 1956, the *Interdepartmental Committee for the Study of Jurisdiction over Federal Areas* within *a State*, commissioned by President Eisenhower, offered

It scarcely needs to be said that unless there has been a transfer of jurisdiction (1) pursuant to clause 17 by a Federal acquisition of land with State consent, or (2) by cession from the State to the Federal government, or unless the Federal Government possess no legislative jurisdiction over any area within a State, such jurisdiction being for exercise entirely by the States subject to non-interference by the State with federal functions, and subject to the free exercise by the

Federal Government of rights with respect to the use, protection, and disposition of its property.

90) In *Downes v Bidwell*, the Supreme Court stated,

First. The government of the United States was born of the Constitution, and all powers which it enjoys or may exercise must be either derived expressly or by implication from that instrument. Ever then, when an act of any department is challenged because not warranted by the Constitution, the existence of the authority is to be ascertained by determining whether the power has been conferred by the Constitution, either in express terms or by lawful implication, to be drawn from the express authority conferred, or deduced as an attribute which legitimately inheres in the nature of the powers given, and which flows from the character established by the Constitution. In other words, while confined to its constitutional orbit, **the government of the United States is supreme within its lawful sphere**. *182 US 244, 288-289 (1901)*

91) The United States has supreme, general, and exclusive jurisdiction over what it controls. We must conclude the Federal Government has authority over taxpayers engaged in a federally excisable privilege *within the United States*. These taxpayers have a federal status. The tax code applies to such *persons*.

Taxpayer: The term "taxpayer" **means any person subject** to any internal revenue tax. *26 USC 7701(a)(14), Subtitle F Procedure and Administration, Chapter 79, Definitions*

92) The United States Court of Claims stated,

Revenue Laws relate to taxpayers and not to non-taxpayers. The latter are without their scope. **No procedures are prescribed for non-taxpayers and no attempt is made to annul any of their Rights or Remedies in due course of law**. With them Congress does not assume to deal and they are neither the subject nor the object of the federal revenue laws. *Economy Plumbing & Heating v U.S., 470 F2d. 585 (1972)*

The revenue laws are a code or system in regulation of tax assessment and collection. They relate to taxpayers, and not to nontaxpayers. The latter are without their scope. No procedure is prescribed for nontaxpayers, and no attempt is made to annul any of their rights and remedies in due course of law. **With them Congress does not assume to deal, and they are neither of the subject nor the object of the revenue laws**... *Long v Rasmussen, 281 F. 236 (1922)*

93) Who are "non taxpayers?" Who is outside or without the United States? The Court stated:

The right to follow any of the common occupations of life is an inalienable right. *Butchers' Union, etc., Co., v Crescent City, etc., Co. 111 US 746, 762 (1883)*

It has been well said that "**The property which every man has in his own labor**, as it is the original foundation of all other property, so it **is the most sacred and inviolable**. The patrimony of the poor man lies in the strength and dexterity of his own hands, and to hinder his employing this strength

144

and dexterity in what manner he thinks proper, without injury to his neighbor, is a plain violation of that most sacred property. *Pg 757*

Included in **the right of personal liberty and the right of private property** – partaking of the nature of each – **is the right to make contracts for the acquisition of property**. Chief among such contracts is that of **personal employment**, by which **labor and other services are exchanged for money or other forms of property**. If this right be struck down or arbitrarily interfered with, there is a substantial impairment of liberty in the long established constitutional sense. *Coppage v Kansas, 236 US 1, 14 (1915)*

94)   Court decisions within two of the several States express this same sentiment.

Since the right to receive income or earnings is a right belonging to every person, this right cannot be taxed as a privilege. *Jack Cole Company v McFarland, Commissioner, 206 Tenn. 694 337 S.W. 2d 453, Supreme Court of Tennessee (1960)*

Note the term *income* is used in a general sense and cannot mean *profit or gain*.

An **income tax is neither a property tax nor a tax on occupations of common right**, but **is an excise**... The **legislature may** declare as "privileged" and **tax** as such for state revenue, those **pursuits not matters of common right**, but **it has no power to** declare as a "privilege" and **tax** for revenue purposes, **occupations** that are **of common right**. _Simms v Ahrens_, 271 SW 720 (1925)

95) A final and compelling citation by the Supreme Court of the United States discloses,

> But the fundamental **rights to life, liberty, and the pursuit of happiness**, considered as individual possessions, are secured by those maxims of constitutional law which are monuments showing the victorious progress of the race in securing to men the blessings of civilization under the reign of just and equal laws, so that, in the famous language of the Massachusetts Bill of Rights, the government of the Commonwealth "may be a government of laws and not of men." For t**he very idea that one man may be compelled to hold his life, or the means of living, or any material right essential to the enjoyment of life, at the mere will of another, seems to be intolerable** in any country **where freedom prevails**, as being the essence of slavery itself. _Yick Wo v Hopkins,_ 118 US 356, 370 (1886)

96) The import of man's natural rights and the concept of limited federal jurisdiction cannot be denied. Moreover, there is a correlation with one's status as to whether or not he is a taxpayer or non taxpayer. How does the United States exercise general or exclusive jurisdiction over Americans within the several States?

97) Regrettably, private business owners serve as unpaid _agents_ who register _employees_ into the federal system. Once _employed_, Americans enter the orbit of the federal government for the collection of the social security tax and the income tax. Out of ignorance and fear, business owners require prospective

employees to complete federal tax forms and Americans ignorantly submit those tax forms.

98)   The completion of federal forms is no small matter. A private business within one of the several States, over which the Federal Government has no jurisdiction, expects the submission of W-2, W-4 forms, among others, as a condition of employment. This volitional, but uninformed decision, accounts for Americans entering within the jurisdiction of the *United States*.

99)   Federal tax forms and the annual reporting of *income* by *employers* become third-party confirmation of *employment* and *income* with the resulting tax liability. The IRS expects all *employees* to submit copies of the W-2 with a 1040 form, which will match the "testimony" (prima facie evidence) of the *employer*. The government expects both the *employer* and *employee* to comply.

100) Note the IRS mission statement:

> Internal Revenue Manual (I.R.M.) Section 1.1.1.1 (02-26-1999) IRS Mission and Basic Organization
> (1)   The IRS Mission: Provide America's **taxpayers** top quality service by helping them **understand and meet their tax responsibilities** and by applying the tax law with integrity and fairness **to all**.

Article 1, Section 8   Internal Revenue Code   United States property
Taxpayers   Article 1, Section 8, Clause 17   territory and possessions

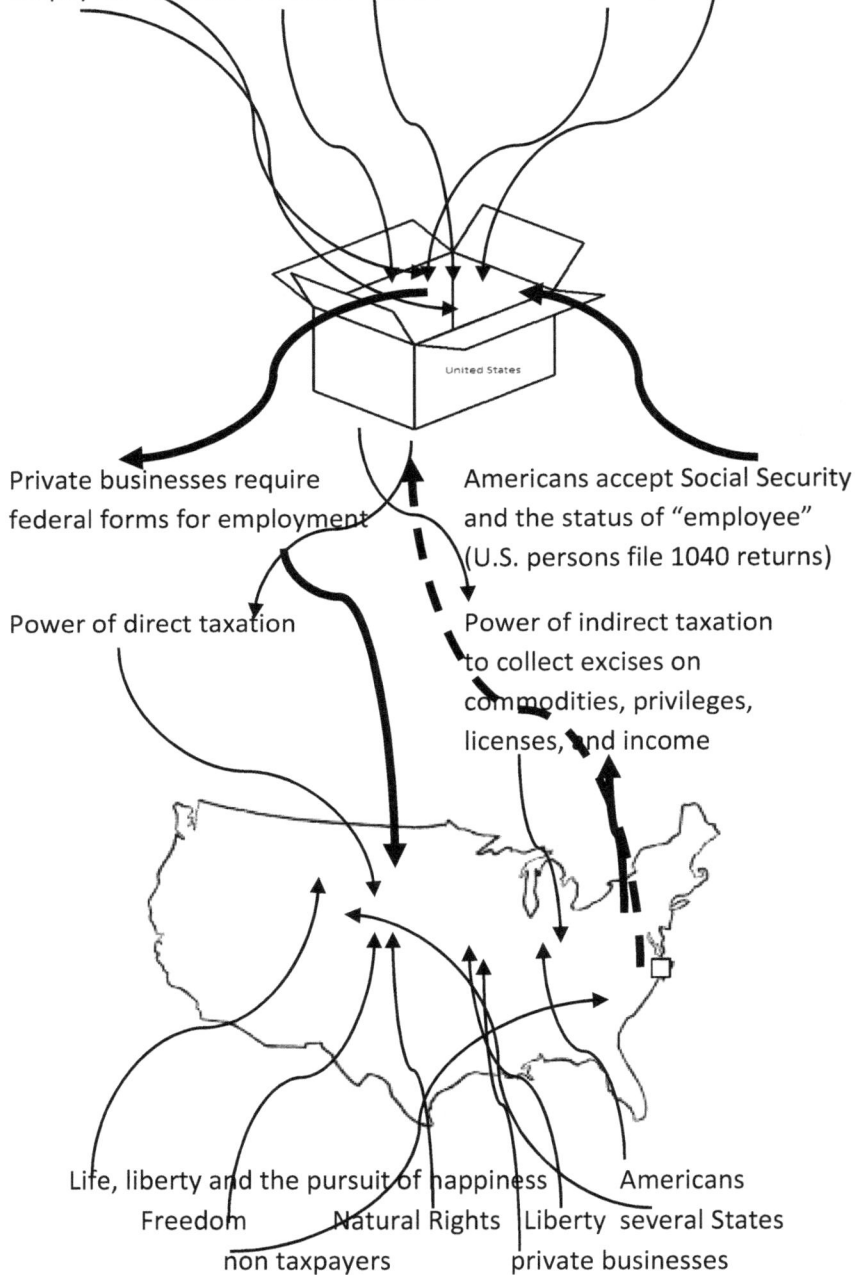

United States

Private businesses require
federal forms for employment

Americans accept Social Security
and the status of "employee"
(U.S. persons file 1040 returns)

Power of direct taxation

Power of indirect taxation
to collect excises on
commodities, privileges,
licenses, and income

Life, liberty and the pursuit of happiness   Americans
Freedom   Natural Rights Liberty several States
non taxpayers   private businesses

148

Tax Code and Regulations

101) Since the code and regulations are complex, our discussion will give us greater understanding than most lawyers possess.

[We must note here, as a matter of judicial knowledge, that most lawyers have only scant knowledge of tax law.] _Bursten v United States_, 395 F 2d 976, 981 (5th Cir 1968)

102) The following text qualifies that not all are required to have a taxpayer identification number.

Taxpayer identifying numbers are not required for foreign governments, **nonresident aliens not engaged in trade or business within the United States**, international organizations and foreign corporations not engaged in trade or business and not having an office or place of business or a financial or paying agent within the United States, and **other persons** or organizations as **may be exempted from furnishing such numbers** under regulations of the Internal Revenue Service _31 CFR 306.10 fn 2_

103) Now consider:

Internal Revenue Manual, Section 4.10.7.2.8 (01-01-2006)
1. **IRS Publications explain the law** in plain language **for taxpayers** and their advisors. They typically highlight changes in the law, provide examples illustrating Service positions, and include worksheets. Publications are nonbinding on the Service and do not necessarily cover all positions for a given issue. While a good source of general

information, publications should not be cited to sustain a position.

A **domestic corporation is one organized or created in the United States, including** only the **States and the District of Columbia**, or under the law of the United States or of any State or Territory. **A foreign corporation is one which is not domestic.** A domestic corporation is a resident corporation even though it does no business and owns no property in the United States. **A foreign corporation engaged in trade or business within the United States is** referred to in the regulations in this chapter as **a resident foreign corporation,** and **a foreign corporation not engaged in a trade or business within the United States**, as **a nonresident foreign corporation.** A partnership engaged in trade or business within the United States is referred to in the regulations in this chapter as a resident partnership, and a partnership not engaged in trade or business within the United States, as a nonresident partnership. Whether a partnership is to be regarded as resident or nonresident is not determined by the nationality or residence of its members or by the place in which it was created or organized. *26 CFR 301.7701-5 Domestic, foreign, resident, and nonresident persons.*

104) The tax code creates and confirms the presumption of a tax liability of those with identifying numbers.

Sec 6109. Identifying numbers.
(a) Supplying identifying numbers
When required by regulations prescribed by the Secretary:
(1) Inclusion in returns

Any person required under the authority of this title **to make a return**, statement, or other document shall include such identifying number as may be prescribed for securing proper identification of such person. *26 USC, Subtitle F Procedure and Administration, Chapter 61 Information and Returns, Subchapter B Miscellaneous Provisions, Section 6109*

105) So, who is required to "make returns?"

Sec 6012 Persons required to make returns of income
(a) General rule
Returns with respect to income taxes under Subtitle A shall be made by the following:
(1)(A)
Every individual having for the taxable year **gross income** which equals or exceeds the exemption amount... *26 USC, Subtitle F Procedures and Administration, Chapter 61 Information and Returns, Subchapter A Returns and Records, Part II Tax Returns or Statements, subpart B Income Tax Returns*

106) *Persons* are expected to secure an identifying number which a return requires. The instructions on the SS-4 Form (Application for Employer Identification Number) states,

Do I need an EIN
File Form SS-4 if the applicant entity does not already have an EIN but **is required** to show an EIN on any return, statement or other document. For example, a sole proprietorship or self-employed farmer who establishes a qualified retirement plan or is required to file excise,

employment, alcohol, tobacco, or firearms, must have an EIN. A partnership, corporation, REMIC (real estate mortgage investment conduit), nonprofit organization (church, club, etc), or farmers' cooperative must use an EIN for any tax-related purpose even if the entity does not have employees.

107) Note the language in the Privacy Act Notice (SS-4 Form).

We ask for the information on this form to carry out the Internal Revenue laws for the United States. **We need it to comply with section 6109** and the regulations thereunder, **which generally require the inclusion of an employer identification number** (EIN) on certain returns, statements, or other documents filed with the Internal Revenue Service

108) The appearance of liability is created while leaving but the faintest suggestion that it is not for everyone. This is the stated purpose of the W-9 Form. Note the words "only if."

A person who is required to file an information return with the IRS must obtain your correct taxpayer identification number (TIN) to report, for example, income paid to you, real estate transactions, mortgage interest you paid, acquisition or abandonment of secured property, cancellation of debt, or contributions you made to an IRA. U.S person. **Use Form W-*9 only if you are a U.S. person (including a resident alien)*,** to provide your correct TIN to the person requesting it...

109) The code stipulates that employers are liable for the tax. But who is the employer, after all, and from within what jurisdiction?

3403. Liability for tax.

The **employer shall be liable** for the payment of the tax required to be deducted and withheld under this chapter, and shall not be liable to any person for the amount of any such payment. *26 USC, Subtitle C – Employment Taxes, Chapter 24 – Collection of Income at Source on Wages, Subchapter A – Withholding from wages*

The *employer*, with its EIN, has a responsibility to pay the IRS the requisite amount due and owed for all *employees*.

110) The definition of "employee" in "Liability for tax" is:

3401 – Definitions.

(c) For purposes of this chapter, the term **"employee" includes an officer, or elected official of the United States, a State or any political subdivision thereof, or instrumentality of any one or more of the foregoing**. The term "employee" also includes an officer of a corporation.

The significance of this definition cannot be overstated. We see that Americans or Citizens of the several States are not included. Yet, *employees* of the *United States* or a *State* are and would be within the list and definition. Compare this definition with the Income Tax Act of 1862. Clearly, *employees* enter the jurisdiction of the *United States*. The regulations reveal how.

301.6109 - Identifying numbers.

(a) In general – (1) Taxpayer identifying numbers – (i) Principle types. **There are several types of taxpayer identifying numbers** that include the following: **social security numbers**, Internal Revenue Service (IRS) **individual**

taxpayer identification numbers, IRS adoption taxpayer identification numbers, and employer identification numbers. *26 CFR Internal Revenue, Chapter 1 – Internal Revenue Service, Department of the Treasury, Subchapter F – Procedures and Administration, Miscellaneous Provisions*

111) The next section states the mandate to provide the number.

(b) Requirement to furnish one's number – (1) **U.S. persons. Every U.S. person who makes under this title a return,** statement, or other document **must furnish its own taxpayer identifying number** as required by the forms and accompanying instructions. A U.S. person whose number must be included on a document filed by another person must give the taxpayer identifying number so required to the other person on request.

Is there any doubt that a *U.S. person* is required to provide *its* number? Is there any doubt that anyone with a *taxpayer number* is a *U.S. person*? Is there any doubt the *United States* has a presumption that each the above is true when Americans subscribe to a federal status or benefit?

112) Section C of the same subchapter addresses the need to furnish the number of another.

(C) Requirement to furnish another's number. **Every person required** under this title to make a return, statement, or other document must furnish such taxpayer identifying numbers of such other persons...

Note the combining of requirements of employers and employees, which will become more evident as we proceed.

113) Referring back to 301.6109-1(b)(1) *U.S. persons*, note:

> ... For provisions dealing specifically **with the duty of employees with respect to their social security numbers**, see Section 31.6011(b)-2(a) and (b) of this chapter (Employment Tax Regulations). For provisions dealing specifically with the duty of employers with respect to employer identification numbers, see Section 31.6011(b)-1 of this chapter (Employment Tax Regulations).

114) The tax regulations correspond to sections of the tax code. Section 26 CFR 31.6011 corresponds to 26 USC 6011.

> Section 6011 General Requirement of return, statement, or list.
> (b) Identification of Taxpayer
> The Secretary is authorized to require such identification with respect to **persons subject to the taxes imposed** by chapter 21 or chapter 24 as is necessary or helpful in securing proper identification of such persons. *26 USC, Subchapter F Procedure and Administration, Chapter 61 Information and Returns, Subchapter A Returns and Records, Part II Tax Returns or Statements, Subpart A General Requirement*

Note the consistent emphasis on *persons*. Chapter 21 concerns "Federal Insurance Contributions Act" and chapter 24 concerns "Collection of Income Tax at Source."

115) Section 31.6011(b)-1 concerns *employers* and their identification numbers.

> 31.6011(b)-1 Employers' identification numbers
> (a) Requirement of application – (1) In general – (i) Before October 1, 1962. Except as provided in paragraph (b) of this section, **every employer** who... has in his employ one or more **individuals in employment for wages subject to the taxes** imposed by the Federal Insurance Contributions Act, but who prior to such day has neither secured an account number nor made application therefor, **shall make an application on Form SS-5** for an account number.

116) Two purposes of taxation are cited, Social Security and withholding of income tax from *wages*. When employees are taxed, there are two amounts deducted and paid, one for which the employee is responsible for FICA and one for the employer for the relation of employment.

117) Before we finish with section 301.6109-1 "Identifying numbers," consider the code sections which apply to "self-employment," and the income tax under Subtitle A.

> Sec 1401. Rate of Tax.
> (a) Old-age, survivors, and disability insurance.
> In addition to other taxes, there shall be imposed for each taxable year, on the **self-employment income of every individual**, a tax equal to the following percent of the amount of the self-employment income for such taxable year:... *26 USC, Subtitle A Income Taxes, Chapter 2 Tax on self-employment income*

Sec 1402. Definitions

(a) Net earnings from self-employment

The term "net earnings from self-employment" means the gross income derived by an **individual from any trade or business** carried on by such individual... Id.

118) We see a distinction between the self-employed and the employed. The main difference concerns receipt of *wages* by the employed and "gains, profits and income" by the self-employed.

Sec 6041 Information at Source

(a) Payments of $600 or more

All **persons engaged in a trade or business** and making payment in the course of such **trade or business to another person** of rent, salaries, wages, premiums, annuities, compensations, remunerations, emoluments, or other fixed or determinable gains, profits, and income... shall render a true and accurate return... *26 USC, Subchapter F Information and Returns, Subchapter A Returns and Records, Part III Information Returns, Subpart B Information concerning transactions with other persons*

119) Once again, the use of the term *person* is notable. Consider that section 6041 A, which deals with "Returns regarding payments of remuneration for services and direct sales."

Sec 6041 A. Returns regarding payments of remuneration for services and direct sales. (a) Returns regarding payments of remuneration for services. If – (1) any service recipient engaged in a **trade or business pays in the course of such trade or business during any calendar year remuneration to any person for services performed by such person**, and

157

(2) the aggregate of such remuneration paid to such person during such calendar year is $600 or more, **then the service recipient shall make a return**... Id.

The government expects the "recipient" of a "service" done by the "self-employed" person engaged in a "trade or business" to provide third party confirmation that the *self-employed person* received the remuneration paid. This practice is consistent with the *employer* reporting the receipt of *wages* by *employee*.

120) The legal term *trade or business* is limited in scope and serves a particular purpose.

> Sec 7701. Definitions
> (a) When used in this title, where not otherwise distinctly expressed or manifestly incompatible with the intent thereof –
>
> (26) Trade or Business
> The term "trade or business" **includes the performance of the functions of a public office**. *26 USC, Subtitle F Procedures and Administration, Chapter 79 Definitions*.

Now, of all possible definitions for this term—a legal term—why is this language used? The obvious answer is to create the liability within the jurisdiction of the tax code of the *United States* for those liable. Note the nature of the class identified—public office. This is consistent with the Income Tax Act of 1862.

121) Consider the definition of "Public Office," which is consistent with "trade or business."

Public office

Essential characteristics of a "public office" are:

Authority conferred by law

Fixed tenure of office, and

Power to exercise some of the sovereign functions of government

Key element of such test is that **"officer is carrying out a sovereign function"**

Essential elements to establish public position as "public office" are:

a) Position **must be created by Constitution, legislature, … or authority conferred by legislature**

b) Portion of **sovereign power of government must be delegated to position**

c) **Duties and power must be defined**, directly or implied, by legislature or…[its] authority

d) **Duties must be performed independently** without control of superior power other than law

e) Position **must have some permanency**. (Black's Law Dictionary, 6ᵗʰ Edition) [brackets added]

122) Note that section 6041 A defines *person* as:

(d) Applications of governmental units.

(1) Treated as persons.

The term "person" **includes any governmental unit** (and any agency or instrumentality thereof).

What is a "governmental unit?" What is an "agency or instrumentality?" Is it possible that *persons* and *U.S. persons* are governmental units within the jurisdiction of the *United States* when they accept a federal status and benefit?

123) Having addressed the receipt of income by the self-employed, consider *wages* received by the *employee*. We already examined the liability of the *employer* to pay the tax under section 3403 and the definition of *employee* under 3401. Let's read the definition of "wages."

> Sec 3401. Definitions.
> (a) Wages.
> For purposes of this chapter, the term wages means all remuneration (other than fees paid to a public official) for services performed by an employee for his employer...

124) Section 3402 addresses the requirement to withhold.

> Sec 3402. Income tax collected at source.
> (a) Requirement of withholding.
> (1) In general.
> Except as otherwise provided in this section, every employer making payments of wages shall deduct and withhold upon such wages a tax determined in accordance with tables or computations procedures prescribed by the Secretary.

125) The following concerning Social Security and Medicaid (FICA) deals with taxes on wages.

> Sec 3101 Rate of tax.
> (a) Old-age, survivors, and disability insurance.
> **In addition to other taxes, there is hereby imposed on the income of every individual a tax** equal to the percentage of the wages (as defined in section 3121(a)) received by him with respect to employment (as defined in section 3121(b))... *26 USC, Subtitle C Employment Taxes and*

*Collection of Income Tax, Chapter 21 Federal Insurance
Contributions Act, Subtitle A Tax on Employees*

Sec 3121 Definitions
(a) Wages
For purposes of this chapter, the term **"wages" means all
remuneration for employment,** including cash value of all
remuneration (including benefits) paid in any medium other
than cash... Id., *Subchapter C General provisions.*
(b) Employment
For the purposes of this chapter, **the term "employment"
means any service**, of whatever nature, performed
(A) **by an employee for the person employing him**,
irrespective of the citizenship or residence of either,
(ii) on **or in connection with an American vessel of
American aircraft**... or (B) outside the United States **by a
citizen or resident of the United States as an employee
for an American employer** (as defined in subsection (h))

Legal terms have controlled meanings to the exclusion of general
application. Everyone and everywhere within the several States
do not and cannot apply. Yet, the contrary appearance may be
presumed. Note, under 3121, "citizenship" or "residence" does
not matter as long as it is within the United States. Also note the
"citizen or resident of the United States" is relevant "outside of
the United States," for an "American employer."

126) Consider "American employer" in subsection h.

(h) American employer
For the purposes of this chapter, the term "American
employer" means an employer which is –

(1) the **United States** or an instrumentality thereof,

(2) **an individual who is a resident** of the United States,

(3) **a partnership**, if two-thirds or more of the partners are residents of the United States, or

(4) **a trust**, if all of the trustees are residents of the United States, or

(5**) a corporation** organized under the laws of the United States or of any State

We have a list—*instrumentality, individual and resident*-among those already discussed. It is noteworthy that *American employer* is not simply defined as "any and all businesses within the 'United States' or within the 'several States' that employ an employee." Congress could not do so because *American employer* is not what we expect. *American employer* is only defined with its qualifiers and their limited application. Does *American employer* appear to be the *United States* Government and *its* agencies, etc.?

127) Referring to 26 CFR 1.1441-1, we have the definition of "individual," as well as "withholding," "foreign person," and "U.S. person." The term *individual* is defined as two subclasses—*alien individuals and nonresident alien individuals*. We must conclude that, by virtue of the language used, for the purposes of the federal income tax and the tax code, the term *individual* is limited.

Consider an obvious point. Once the Social Security scheme and relation of employment were established as taxable by excise, were all Americans liable for the tax simply because they were *individuals* in the common usage of the word? Social Security was voluntary and not everyone accepted the status or benefit or entered the *relation of employment*. Moreover, if only government workers were and are *employees*, the limits of the class of *individual* are presumed to be greater than it is. Note the following regulation which defines *individual*.

26 CFR Internal Revenue
Chapter 1 Internal Revenue Service, Department of the Treasury
Subchapter A – Internal revenue
Part 1 – Income taxes
Nonresident aliens and Foreign Corporations
1.1441-1 Requirement for the deduction and withholding of tax on payments to **foreign persons**
(c) Definitions – (1) Withholding. The term withholding means the deduction and withholding of tax at the applicable rate from the payment.
(2) Foreign and U.S. person. The term **foreign person means a nonresident alien individual**, a foreign corporation, a foreign trust, a foreign estate, and **any other person that is not a U.S. person** described in the next sentence. Solely for the purposes of the regulations under chapter 3 of the Internal Revenue Code, the term foreign person also means, with respect to a payment by a withholding agent, **a foreign branch of a U.S. person** that furnishes an intermediary withholding certificate described in paragraph (e)(3)(ii) of this section. Such a branch continues to be a U.S. payor for purposes of chapter 61 of the Internal Revenue Code. See 1.6049-5 (c)(4). **A U.S person is a person described in section 7701(a)(30), the U.S. government (including an agency or instrumentality thereof), a State (including an agency or instrumentality thereof), or the District of Columbia (including an agency or instrumentality thereof).**
(3) Individual – (i) Alien individual. The term **alien individual**

means an individual who is not a citizen or a national of the United States. See 1.1-1(c).

(ii) Nonresident alien individual. The term nonresident alien individual **means a person described in section 7701(b)(1)(B), an alien individual who is a resident of a foreign country** under the residence article of an income tax treaty and 301.7701(b)-7(a)(1) of this chapter, **or** an alien individual who is **a resident of Puerto Rico, Guam, the Commonwealth of Northern Mariana Islands, the U.S. Virgin Islands, or American Samoa** as determined under 301.7701(b)-1(d) of this chapter. An alien individual who has made an election under section 6013(g) or (h) to be treated as a resident of the United States is nevertheless treated as a nonresident alien individual for purposes of withholding under chapter 3 of the Code and the regulations thereunder.

128) Consider the definition of *individual* in 5 USC 552(a):

Government of the United States (including survivor benefits). 5 USC 552a. Records maintained on individuals... (2) the term "individual" means **a citizen of the United States or an alien** lawfully admitted for permanent residence:

129) Credence must be granted for the purposeful use of terms under Congressional Acts that define or classify terms. Notably, Congress passed The Classification Act of 1923,

An Act To provide for the classification of civilian positions within the District of Columbia and in the field services.

130) This Act defines "department," "position," "employee," "service," and "compensation."

> The term "department" means an executive department of the United States Government...
> The term "position" means a specific **civilian office or employment**...
> The term "employee" means **any person... in a position**...
> The term "service" means the broadest division of related **offices and employments**.
> The term "class" means a group of positions...
> The term "compensation" means any salary, wage, fee, allowance, or other emolument paid to an **employee for service in a position**.

This Act clearly shows the deliberate intent to classify, define, or otherwise limit terms of the *United States* for its usage alone. Not surprisingly, this Act became The Classification Act of 1949, which eventually became Title 5, "Government Organization and Employees." The point cannot be any more obvious. Acts and codes largely apply to the *United States* and its *States* and what is within its jurisdiction. By the context of terms, we may reconcile that those who enter the relationship of employment with the use of federal forms or accept a federal status or benefits, like Social Security, are *within the jurisdiction of the United States*.

131) Consider the definition of "employee" in the regulations.

> 31.3401(c) Employee. The term **"employee" includes every individual performing services if the relationship between him and the person for whom he performs such services is the legal relationship of employer and employee. The term**

includes officers and employees whether elected or appointed, of the United States, a State, Territory, or any political subdivision thereof, or the District of Columbia, or any agency or instrumentality of the foregoing. *26 CFR Internal Revenue, Chapter 1 Internal Revenue Service, Department of the Treasury, subchapter C Employment Taxes and Collection of Income at Source, Subpart E Collection of Income Tax at Source*

Does this definition apply to everyone? Does it apply to all those who work? Does it apply only to those who enter the *United States* for the purpose of the Social Security Act? We can rest assured that those engaged in a "legal relationship of employer and employee" are affected, as well as those officials employed by the United States involved in a "trade or business."

American employer   EIN, SSN, TIN   Wages   Trade or business
FICA   withholding   Persons required to make returns   Employers
taxpayers employees   Residents individuals   United States persons
1040 forms W-2, W-4, 1099 forms

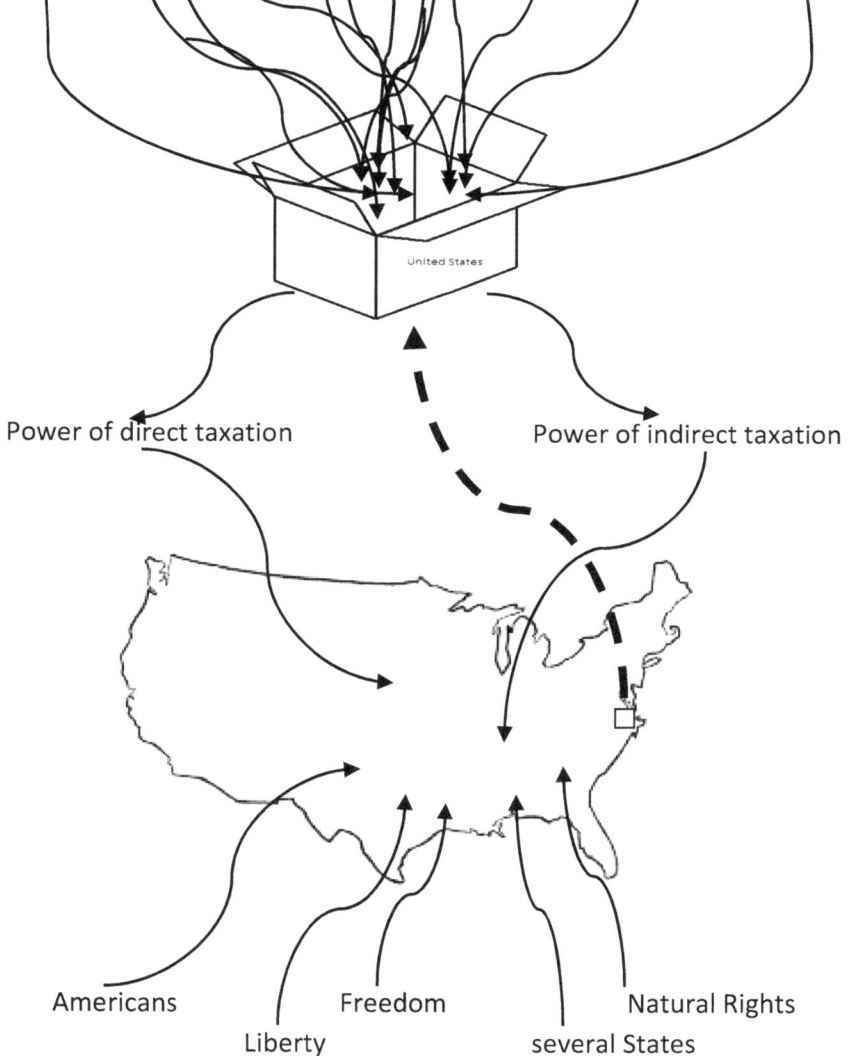

Power of direct taxation   Power of indirect taxation

Americans   Freedom   Natural Rights
        Liberty   several States

Prima Facie Evidence

132) As a practical matter, those who are legally liable for the federal income tax or the income tax associated with Social Security testify annually as to the *income* they earn, the amount owed in taxes or any refund expected. *Taxpayers* certify under penalty of perjury that they are *U.S. persons* filing a 1040 *U.S. Individual* income tax return. The initial filing, as with the submission of any and all tax forms for FICA, is prima facie evidence one is liable.

133) Prima facie evidence is

> **Evidence** which, if unexplained or uncontradicted, is **sufficient to sustain a judgment** in favor of the issue which support, but **which may be contradicted by other evidence.** *Black's Law Dictionary, 5th Ed.*

134) The significance of the filing of one's first 1040 tax form or W-2 and W-4 form, which begins withholding, was reflected by the U.S. Court of Appeals, 9th Circuit, in <u>Morse v United States</u>, 494 F 2d, 876, 880 (1974). The court considered whether or not the citizen was in the legal status of *taxpayer*.

> Accordingly, when **returns were filed** in Mrs. Morse's name **declaring income** to her for 1944 and 1945, and making her potentially liable for the tax due on that income, **she became a taxpayer** within the meaning of the Internal Revenue Code.

The court established that Morse became a *taxpayer*. She became a *U.S. person* when she voluntarily filed her first income tax return thirty years earlier. The government operated under the presumption that she was still a *taxpayer*. Mrs. Morse never rebutted the presumption or prima facie evidence.

135) Consider the words of Assistant United States Attorney, Samuel H. Pillsbury, in <u>United States v Burns</u>, who clearly showed he had an understanding of the term *voluntary*.

> And it never occurred to you that perhaps they had a somewhat **different meaning of the word "voluntary,"** that perhaps they meant **the** actual **initial payment of the taxes or** the **permission to withhold funds**, did it? *Cr-85-122-EF (1985)*

136) With the voluntary filing of tax forms, Americans offer testimony that they are *taxpayers* subject to the tax code. Moreover, these forms are signed under penalty of perjury and serve as prima facie evidence in court, justifying a finding that an American is no longer *without the United States* as a free man exercising his right to labor and earnings, both of which are property. The opposite is true; courts conclude that Americans are *U.S. persons* within the *United States*, subject to federal excise taxes by their own confession.

137) "Taxpayer" is defined as "any person subject to any internal revenue tax." It does not state that a taxpayer is any person who pays the tax. The presumption is created by acts which makes one a person liable, which is legally sufficient for the government. The IRS naturally expects continued filings of tax returns with or without payment.

138) A *taxpayer* has the same legal status as a "trust, estate, partnership, association, company or corporation," which are all government-created *persons*, as defined under section 7701 of the tax code. These *persons* exist within the scope of the tax laws and purview of the federal government. These *persons* have a federal status and privileges. Does a *taxpayer* lose constitutionally secured rights to all his earnings? We must conclude a *taxpayer* is required to conform to the law like any other "applicant entity" *within the United States* where the Constitution does not apply.

Consider the definition of "person," which is the first term defined in 26 USC 7701. Then consider "taxpayer."

(a) when used in this title
(1) Person. The term "**person**" shall be construed to mean and include an **individual**, a trust, estate, partnership, association, company or corporation.
(14) Taxpayer. The term "**taxpayer**" means any **person** subject to any internal revenue tax.

Recall the concepts of noscitur a sociis and ejusdem generis and the limits of "includes" and "including." There can be little doubt that the items listed under the term person are creations of the federal government for the purpose of applying the tax code. Even as a status, classification, or title, *individual* is a *person* and, therefore, a *taxpayer*. Why define the commonly accepted word *person* unless there is an intended legal objective?

139) From the court's perspective, when a *taxpayer* is charged criminally for "willful failure to file" tax returns, he is not an American with his rights to his property secured by natural rights. His rights are not free from encroachment by the constraints of the Constitution. Rather, he is a *United States*

person with a legal obligation. The courts will instruct the jury that the defendant is required to file tax returns. Courts tell jurors that this is the law. Within this limited context, the courts are correct.

140) We now have proper context as to the nature of the Internal Revenue Code and the paper scheme which facilitates the collection of information for tax purposes. Americans, without fully informed consent, willingly left the vast expanse of freedom with natural rights within the several States and entered *within the United States*. Be it the *State* of the District of Columbia, Puerto Rico, Guam, or the Virgin Islands, it can be legally substantiated that Americans became *persons within the United States* for purposes of the income tax code.

141) The deliberate use of legal terms and the people's ignorance and fear are reasons Americans have relinquished their freedom and property. Let's conclude that Americans deliberately choose to receive the federal benefit/privilege of Social Security and enter the *relation of employment* or acquire a federal status. Nothing more is needed to create the presumption that they are *taxpayers* and *U.S. persons*. If Americans never accepted such statuses or privileges, the *United States* Government could not presume otherwise. Americans would remain *nontaxpayers without the United States*. Ultimately, Americans acquire a status within a foreign domain—the United States—foreign to the several States, foreign to the land of freedom. And by doing so, they are required to pay a legally legitimate excise tax.

Have you entered within the United States by presumption and the submission of prima facie evidence? Are you incompetent and, thus, within parens patriae oversight of the government?

Permission to withhold funds 5 USC   tax code   Federal privileges
tax regulations   withholding Classification Act of 1923 income tax
return initial payment of tax MRS. MORSE   MR. BURNS Person, trust,
estate, partnership, association, company, corporation

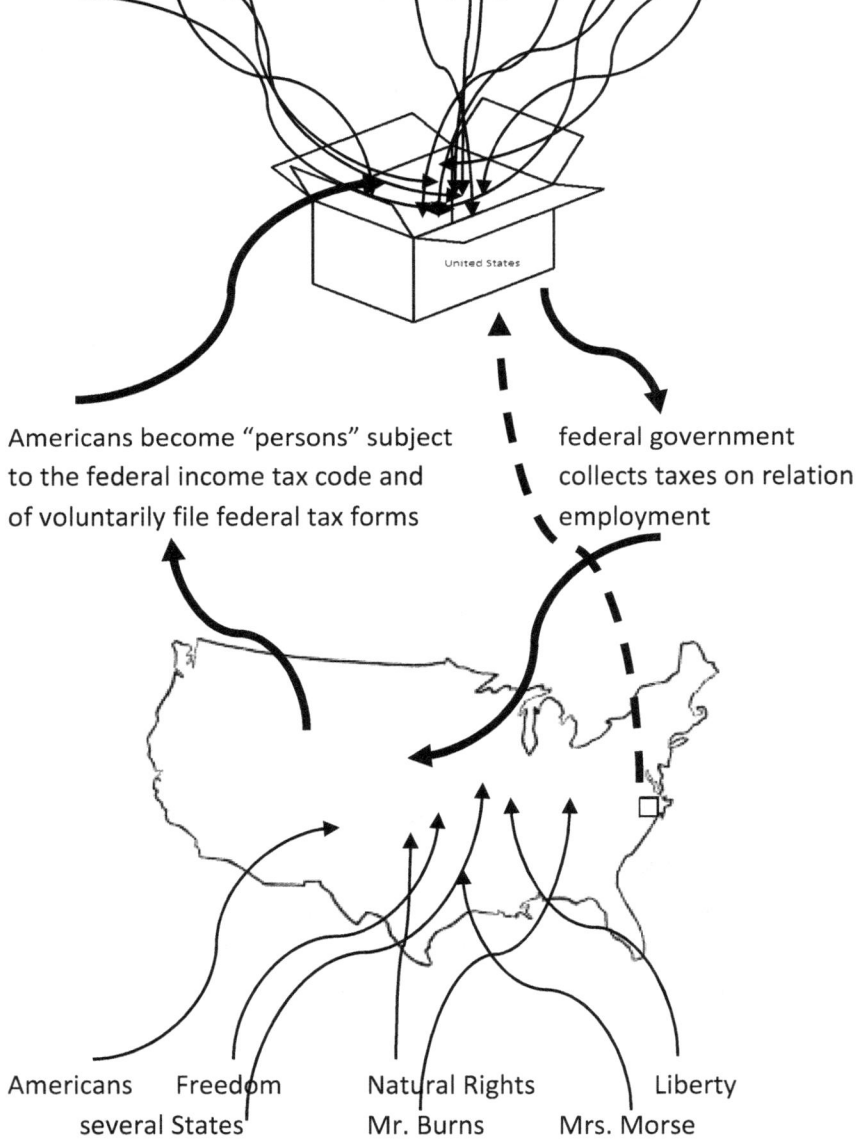

United States

Americans become "persons" subject
to the federal income tax code and
of voluntarily file federal tax forms

federal government
collects taxes on relation
employment

Americans   Freedom
        several States

Natural Rights   Liberty
Mr. Burns   Mrs. Morse

Are You One of Every?

142) Congress could not state the income tax law as:

Every man and woman of legal age, who lives in any of the 50 States or U.S. Territories and possessions, and works for anyone or any class of business, or who works for him or herself, and earns $600.00 or more annually, is hereby subject to a 10% income tax.

The law cannot be this clear since the federal government does not have jurisdiction over Americans within the several States, that is, unless or until Americans agree to the federal tax scheme. The tax code is written to create the appearance of an obligation when it is not mandatory at all.

143) Consider section (d) of 301.6109-1 of the regulations.

301.6109-1 Identifying numbers.
(d) Obtaining a taxpayer identifying number
(1) Social Security number
... **Individuals who are eligible for or do not wish to participate in the benefits of the social security program shall nevertheless obtain a social security number** if they are required to furnish such number pursuant to paragraph (b) of this section

As stated in the letter from Charles Mullen of the Social Security Administration, one is not required to have a number or accept the privilege/benefit Social Security. In 301.6109-1, the use of the term "if" suggests one may not be required to "furnish" the number. Finally, the term "shall" is used—not "required" or "must." While the term, "shall," suggests a mandatory tone, courts have ruled it means "may." Doing so defeats a constitutional conflict. If Congress does not have the authority to require an act, it may allow for one to do so voluntarily.

144) In a footnote to a Supreme Court case, reference is made to Mellinkoff's Dictionary of American Legal Usage, 402-403 (1992), which states "'shall' and 'may' are frequently used as synonyms." Consider that Garner's Dictionary of Modern Legal Usage 939 (2 Ed 1995) states, "courts in virtually every English-speaking jurisdiction have held–by necessity–that shall means may in some contexts and vice versa."

145) Consider Section 6012 of the tax code and the term "shall."

Sec 6012. Persons required to make returns of income.
(a) General rule
Returns with respect to income taxes under subtitle A **shall be made by** the following:
(1)(A) **Every individual** having for the taxable year gross income which equals or exceeds the exemption amount...

The title states, "Persons required **to make** returns of income." Notably, titles to the codes have no binding legal effect and are not law. Consider section 7806 of the tax code.

Sec 7806. Construction of title.
(b) Arrangement and classification.
No inference, implication, or presumption of legislative construction shall be drawn or made by reason of the location or grouping of any particular section or provision or portion of this title, nor shall any table of contents, or similar

outline, analysis, or descriptive matter relating to the contents of this title be given any legal effect.

The code says *every individual shall* make returns. We learned earlier that those *persons* obligated to make a return are those who are within a listing or class of government entities–those with a federal status and liability. They must comply. Yet, in the common usage of the term *individual*, does every man and woman have that same obligation? *Individuals* are *persons* within a class within the code with a legal tax obligation, which cannot include every human being in America.

We know that not all *individuals* (people) are liable to the federal income tax and every *person* who has the obligation would include all such *persons* and *individuals*. If all men and women are not liable to make a return, we recognize the practical use of the term *shall*. If people interpret *every* as more than those required, the term *shall* (may) encourages those who are not required to comply. *Shall* skirts any constitutional conflict when those not obligated do so voluntarily without a congressional mandate or force of law.

146) The importance of the term *every* was made by the Supreme Court in 1909, a time which saw the Corporation Excise Act of 1909, the 16th Amendment, and the 1913 Income Tax Act.

> The foregoing considerations would lead, in case of doubt, to a construction of any statute as intended to be confined in its operation and effect to the territorial limits over which the lawmaker has general and legitimate power. "all legislation is prima facie territorial." Ex parte Blain, L.R. 12 CH. Div. 522, 528; State v Carter, 27 N.J.L. 499; People v Merrill, 2 Park. Crim. Rep. 590, 596. Words having universal

scope, such as "every contract in restraint of trade," "every person who shall monopolize," etc., will be taken, as a matter of course, to mean only everyone subject to such legislation, not all that the legislator subsequently may be able to catch. *American Banana Co. v U.S. Fruit*, *213 US 347, 357-358*

147) The Federal Government could not "catch" "every" "person," so it took "every" legal opportunity to create the presumption that more than those liable were actually liable. Even the code offers admissions that not all or *every person* are subject to the tax statutes. Notice the following language concerning the execution of levies. When the IRS seeks to levy a man's earnings from a private employer or bank account, the agency mails an excerpt from the code as justification. Curiously, the IRS sends paragraph (b) and purposely excludes paragraph (a).

> (b) Seizure and sale of property.
> The term "levy" as used in this title includes the power of distraint and seizure by any means. Except as otherwise provided in subsection (e), a levy shall extend only to property possessed and obligations existing at the time thereof. In any case in which the Secretary may levy upon property or rights to property, he may seize and sell such property (whether real or personal, tangible or intangible.) *26 USC, Subtitle F Procedure and Administration, Chapter 64 Collection, Subchapter D Seizure of property for collection of taxes, Part II Levy, Section 6331 Levy and distraint.*

The text appears to be clear. However, as we examine the authority for any levy, we see the limitations of application. Once we understand the content of paragraph (a), we can challenge the meaning and intent and question if levies apply to *every person* or *every individual*.

> (a) Authority of Secretary. If any person liable to pay any tax neglects or refuses to pay the same within 10 days after notice and demand, it shall be lawful for the Secretary to collect such tax (and further sum as shall be sufficient to cover the expenses of the levy) by levy upon all property and right to property (except such property as is exempt under section 6334) belonging to such person or on which there is a lien provided in this chapter for the payment of such tax. **Levy may be made upon the accrued salary or wages of any officer, employee, or elected official, of the United States or the District of Columbia, or any agency or instrumentality of the United States or District of Columbia, by serving a notice of levy on the employer (as defined in section 3401(d)) of such officer, employee, or elected official.** *Id.*

Compare this language with the Income Tax Act of 1862 and the definitions for *trade and business* and *employee* within the tax code and regulations or *public office* in Black's Law Dictionary. We have a rather transparent admission that not *every person* is subject to levy. For, not *every person* is subject to the income tax. If all persons were liable for the tax, the language would clearly state so and the authority to levy would establish the same latitude.

As it stands, the language *includes* only *officers, employees, or elected officials of the United States or the District of Columbia*, those *within* the *United States*, to the exclusion of any and all who are not liable, which pertains to private Americans who do not have a federal status that obligates them to make a return, do not have a Social Security number, have not subscribed to a federal benefit or privilege. Yet, the government presumes those who become *employees* by and through the *relation of employment*, and the submission of federal tax forms, to include the filing of a 1040 federal income tax form, are subject to federal income tax and, therefore, subject to levy.

Relevant Points Revisited

148) We have established:

   a)   The Constitution provides for two forms of taxation – direct and indirect.

   b)   Direct taxes must be apportioned.

   c)   Indirect taxes are excises which must be uniform and paid on a voluntary basis.

   d)   The federal income tax is an excise tax.

   e)   The FICA tax is an income tax.

   f)   The definition of *income* is *profit and gain*. *Income* is also legally defined as *wages* in the code and serve as the measure of the amount of the tax owed.

   g)   The *United States* may only tax within its jurisdiction and power.

   h)   Americans have a right to labor (property) and earnings (property), both of which are an equal exchange.

   i)   With the Income tax of 1862, the government taxed federal *employees*. The income tax law, although more confusing today by design, does the same.

   j)   The federal government passed the Social Security Act in 1935, a program for the *United States* and its territories and possessions. The several States were allowed to participate.

k)   Americans who subscribed to this privilege entered the jurisdiction of the *United States*.

l)   Americans entered the *relation of employment* when they completed federal tax forms.

m)   Americans create the presumption and prima facie evidence that they are subject to the tax.

n)   The Internal Revenue Code is legal and constitutional and concerns the collection of excises.

o)   For the purposes of the tax code, Americans who acquire a federal status or subscribe to federal privileges become *persons, individuals, taxpayers, and U.S. persons*, a class within the *United States* and, therefore, subject to the federal income tax.

The Scope of Federal Law

149) Rule 54c, as once stated under the Federal Rules of Criminal Procedure, confirms the idea that federal laws apply to the *United States* and its property and possessions.

> As used in these rules, the following terms have designated meanings. "Act of Congress" **includes** any act of Congress locally applicable to and in force in the District of Columbia, in Puerto Rico, in a territory or in an insular possession.

150) In 2002, the language of Rule 54c was altered and merged with Rule 1.

> Rule 1(b) is composed of material currently located in Rule 54(C), with several exceptions. First, the reference to an "Act of Congress" has been deleted from the restyled rules; instead the rules use the self-explanatory term "federal statute."

What is the significance of this change? While it is not uncommon for the government to change terms, doing so alters the specific into the general. The term "Act of Congress" was limited in its scope and then changed to "federal statutes," which broadened its perceived application. The meaning of "federal statute" is no different than "Act of Congress." Its scope did not change. This point is extremely relevant.

Those who read Rule 1(b) may inherently conclude that *federal statutes* apply more generally. Since the limited class of the District of Columbia, Puerto Rico, territory, or insular possession is not directly referenced, readers may not likely question limited jurisdiction and, consequently, perceive the increased scope of federal statutes. This is the intended effect. Most do not and would not consider that *Acts of Congress* are limited in scope. Yet, we must recall, Congress has exclusive and general jurisdiction over its own territory. Naturally, an *Act of Congress* or *federal statute* would be enforceable within the District of Columbia, Puerto Rico, territories and insular possessions and those who are *within the United States*.

Consider an example. Let's suppose Congress passed legislation, *an Act of Congress*, a *federal statute*, which required that *citizens of the United States* tape a $1.00 bill to their front doors every Saturday. Would the people of the several States be liable? No. Would the citizens within the District of Columbia, Puerto Rico, territories, and insular possessions be liable? Yes. The Government has complete plenary power over these territories, not the several States.

Is there any difference with the tax laws? The *United States* may pass *federal statutes—Acts of Congress*—which apply to the territories and possessions and *persons* it governs. The fact that Americans enter the *United States* for a status or privilege makes them liable to that federal statute. Pointedly, the *United States* would not reject the $1.00 bills taped to the doors of Citizens within the several States, just as the government will not reject federal tax returns of those without its jurisdiction, those who voluntarily enter its orbit by complying with the *Act of Congress*.

151) If Acts of Congress apply to the federal government, the Social Security Act, the relation of employment, and the making of federal income tax returns apply exclusively to the *United States*. Even the Supreme Court determined that an Act is limited in scope to that which is subject to congressional power.

The Banana Co. Case confined the Sherman Act in its "operation and effect to the territorial limits over which the lawmaker has general and legitimate power." *Steele v Bulova Watch Co., 334 US 280, 291 (1952)*

152) Consider the words of the Supreme Court.

While a statute is presumed to speak from the time of its enactment, it embraces all such **persons or things as subsequently fall within its scope**, and ceases to apply to such thereafter fall without its scope. *De Lima v Bidwell, 182 US 1, 197 (1901)*

The laws of Congress in respect to those matters **do not extend into** the territorial limits of **the states**, but have force only in the District of Columbia, and other places that are within the exclusive jurisdiction of the national government. *CAHA v United States, 152 US 211, 215 (1894)*

In Foley Bros. v Filardo we had occasion to refer to the "canon of construction which teaches that **legislation of Congress**, unless contrary intent appears, is meant to **apply only within the territorial jurisdiction of the United States**..." That presumption, far from being overcome here, is doubly fortified by the language of this statute and legislative purpose underlying it. *United States v Spelar, 338 US 217, 222 (1949)*

153) In a Court of Appeals decision, it was determined that a tax liability could only be created by statute, which is consistent with the limits of an *Act of Congress*.

Moreover, even the collection of **taxes should be exacted from persons upon who a tax liability is imposed by some statute**. _Botta v Scanlon, 288 F 2d 509 (1961)_

154) In Sutherland's Rules of Statutory Construction, an authoritative reference book on the interpretation of statutes, section 66.03 states,

> ... the obligation to pay taxes arises **only by force of legislative action**...

155) In a separate Supreme Court case, consider that,

> **In the interpretation of Statutes** levying taxes **it is the** established **rule** not to exceed their provisions, by implication, beyond the clear import of the language used, or to embrace **matters not specifically pointed out**. In case of doubt they are construed most strongly against the government, and in favor of the citizen. _Gould v Gould, 245 US 151, 153 (1917)_

156) Justice Marshall wrote in McCulloch v Maryland of the limitations of government with respect to taxation.

> **That the power to tax involves the power to destroy; that the power to destroy may defeat and render useless the power to create**; that there is a plain repugnance in conferring on one government a power to control the constitutional measures of another, which other, with respect to those very measures, is declared to be supreme over that which exerts the control, are propositions not to be denied. But all inconsistencies are to be reconciled by the

magic of the word confidence. Taxation, it is said, does not necessarily and unavoidably destroy. To carry it to excess of destruction would be an abuse, to presume which, would banish that confidence which is essential to all government. *4 Wheat 316, 431 (1819)*

Marshall also stated,

No political dreamer was ever wild enough to think of breaking down the lines which separate the States and compounding them into one common mass. *Id., 403*

The full weight of the McCulloch decision is transparent with Marshall's continued insight.

It may be objected to this definition, that the power of taxation is confined to the people and property of a State. **It may be exercised upon every object brought within its jurisdiction**. This is true, but to what source do we trace this right? It is obvious, that it is incident of sovereignty, and it is co-extensive with that to which it is an incident. **All subjects over which the sovereign power of a State extends, are objects of taxation; but those over which it does not extend, are, upon the soundest principles, exempt from taxation. This proposition may almost be pronounced self-evident**.

The sovereignty of a state extends to everything which exists by its own authority, or is **introduced by its permission**... *Id., 429*

Americans were "introduced" to the income tax by "permission" of congressional authority to receive a federal classification and privileges subject to excise, *within the United States*.

> The difficulties arising out of our dual form of government and the opportunities for differing opinions concerning the relative rights of state and national governments are many; but for a very long time **this court has steadfastly adhered to the doctrine that the taxing power of Congress does not extend to the states or their political subdivisions**. The same basic reasoning which leads to that conclusion, we think, requires the limitation upon the power which springs from the bankruptcy clause. United States v Butler, supra. *Ashton v Cameron County Water Improvement District No. 1, 298 US 513 (1936)*

> It is no longer open to question that the general government, unlike the states, Hammer v Dagenhart, 247 US 251, 275, 38 S. Ct 529, 3 A.L.R. 649, Ann.Cas. 1918E724, possesses **no inherent power in respect of the internal affairs of the states**; and emphatically not with regard to legislation. *Carter v Carter Coal Co., 298 US 238, 56 S. Ct 855 (1936)*

157) With respect to federal jurisdiction and Acts of Congress, consider the following definition of "State" as cited in the income tax regulations.

> 31.3121(e)-1 State, United States, citizen
> (a) When used in the regulations in this subpart, **the term "State" includes the District of Columbia, the Commonwealth of Puerto Rico, the Virgin Islands, the**

territories of Alaska and Hawaii before their admission as states, and (when used with respect to services performed after 1960) Guam and American Samoa. *26 CFR, Chapter 1 Internal Revenue Service, Department of the Treasury, Subchapter C Employment, taxes and collection of income tax at source, Subpart B Federal Insurance Contributions Act, General provisions.*

The definition in 31.3121(e) is supported by the following:

(1) **The term State (except when used in section 531) includes Alaska, Hawaii, and the District of Columbia.**
(2) **The term United States when used in a geographical sense means the States, Alaska, Hawaii and the District of Columbia** - *Social Security Act of 1935, Title XI – General Provisions, Section 1101(a)*

Why is there a need to define *State, United States, or citizen*? With the concepts of noscitur a sociis and ejusdem generis and the use of the terms *includes and including*, are those several States, which do not consent to the Social Security Act, which are not included, beholden to the Act? Would such States, therefore, be within the definition of *State* when used in the regulations in this subpart? Are Citizens obligated? In light of the decisions of the Supreme Court, the question is easily answered with a degree of certainty. When the several States voluntarily agreed to participate, did these States enter *within the United States*? Notably, Alaska and Hawaii were *States* of the *United States* as *territories* before entering the Union of several States.

There is a canon of legislative construction which teaches Congress that, unless a contrary intent appears **[legislation]**

is meant to apply only within the territorial jurisdiction of the United States. _U.S. v Spelar_, _338 US 217, 222 (1949)_

The canon of construction which teaches that legislation of Congress, unless a contrary intent appears, is meant to apply only within the territorial jurisdiction of the United States, Blackmer v United States, supra, at 437, is a valid approach whereby unexpressed congressional intent may be ascertained. It is based on the assumption that Congress is primarily concerned with domestic conditions. Foley Brothers, Inc. v Filardo, 336 US 281 (1949)

158) Most Americans are under the impression that the _federal taxing statute_ requires them to pay the income tax. If Americans volunteer, this impression is correct. If Americans did not voluntarily accept the federal benefit or status, the reverse is true. Imagine an American never requesting a Social Security Number, never completing federal tax forms relating to employment, or submitting a 1040 form. He would not have created the initial presumption or prima facie evidence that he was a _taxpayer_ within a _State within the United States_ subject to an _Act of Congress,_ a federal statute with limited scope.

159) With everything discussed, please permit an unexpected twist. How many Americans would subscribe to the benefit of Social Security if they knew it was not a _contract_ and the benefits could be denied? Additionally, would Americans subscribe knowing the _United States_ could terminate or eliminate the program while Americans could not terminate their own involvement, as claimed by the Federal Government?

...railroad benefits, like **social security benefits, are not contractual and may be altered or even eliminated** at any time. _United States Railroad Retirement Board v Fritz, 449 US 166 (1980)_

We must conclude that a **person covered by the Act has not such a right in benefit payments...** This is not to say, however, that **Congress may exercise its power to modify the statutory scheme free of all constitutional constraint.** _Flemming v Nestor, 363 US 603 (1960)_

160) Now what do you think about the scope of the Social Security Act, an _Act of Congress_?

Every person exclusive territorial jurisdiction Federal privileges
      tax regulations   withholding   Every individual
required to file federal income tax returns   Introduced by its
permission   persons MR. BURNS - taxpayer MRS. MORSE - taxpayer

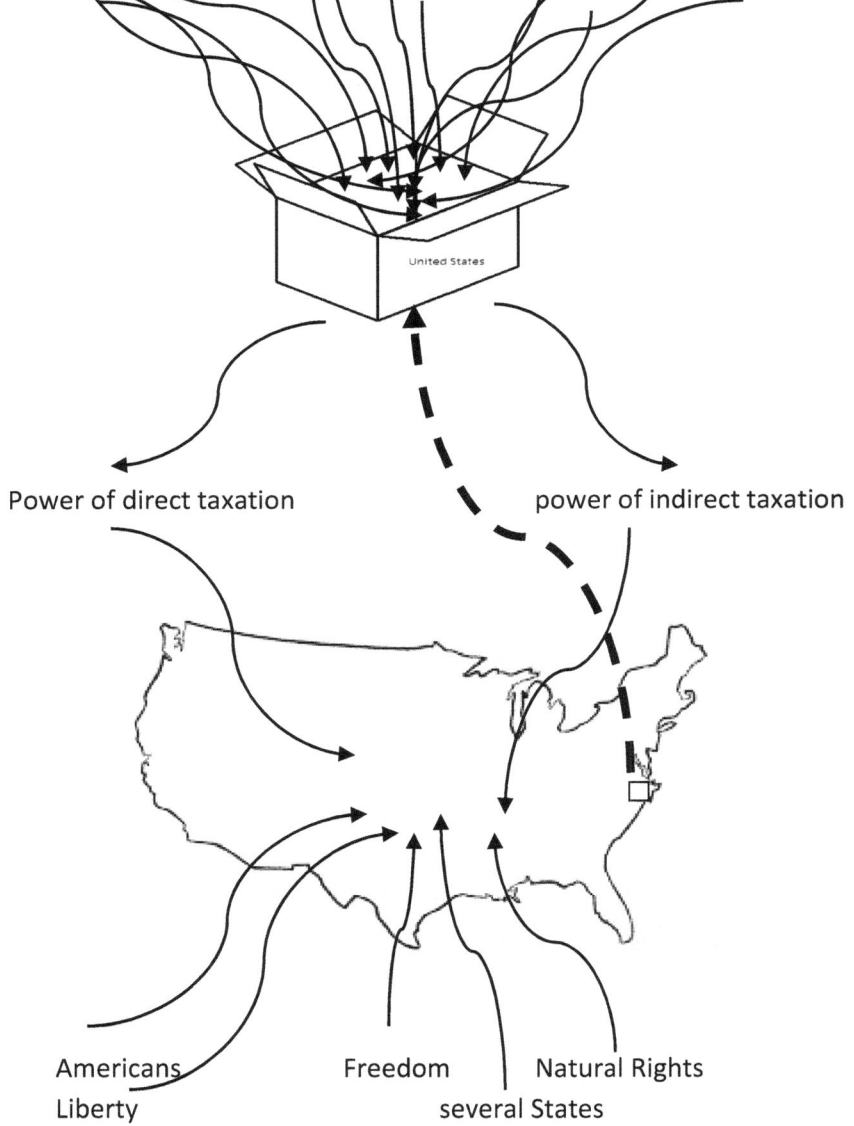

United States

Power of direct taxation   power of indirect taxation

Americans   Freedom   Natural Rights
Liberty   several States

A Matter of Presumption

161) Are Americans victims of fraud or constructive fraud?

> Fraud – a knowing misrepresentation of the truth or concealment of a material fact to induce another to his detriment. *Black's Law Dictionary, 9th Ed.*

> Constructive Fraud – Unintentional deception or misrepresentation that causes injury to another. *Id.*

Was the tax code intentionally written and rewritten with such complexity so as to exclude the truth? If so, the people were and are deceived. If Americans were fully informed, would they have created the presumption or prima facie evidence of a federal income tax liability?

162) Consider the Supreme Court decision in <u>Pennhurst State School v Halderman</u>.

> … however, legislation enacted pursuant to the spending power is much in the of a contract: in return for federal funds, the States agree to comply with federally imposed conditions. **The legitimacy of Congress' power to legislate** under the spending power thus **rests on whether the State voluntarily and knowingly accepts the terms** of the "contract." *451 US 1, 17*

In <u>Pennhurst</u>, the Court cites <u>Charles Steward Machine Co. v Davis</u>, the very case which established the nature of the relation of employment and the limited scope of the Social Security Act. The Court continued by stating,

There can, of course, **be no knowing acceptance if a State is unaware of the conditions or is unable to ascertain what is expected of it**. Accordingly, **if Congress intends to impose a condition** on the grant of federal moneys, **it must do so unambiguously**. By insisting that Congress speak with a clear voice, we enable **the States** to **exercise their choice knowingly, cognizant of their participation**.

163) We can easily draw a parallel to the unforeseen circumstances in which Americans find themselves. Although Pennhurst applies to the States, did not the people enter into a "contract" of sorts without fully informed consent? Most subscribed to Social Security with the perception that it was the *law*. Clearly, Americans could not have had a

> knowing acceptance if [a people is] unaware of the conditions or unable to ascertain [the repercussions of their decision.]

Had the tax code been clearly written or adequately explained, the people would have

> exercised their choice knowingly, cognizant of the consequences of their participation.

As it stands, the people, the very reservoir of power in America, those the government serves, exchange a natural right for a federal status or benefit. This is not the prudent decision an informed, self-reliant, and free people would make.

> "It is apparent" this court said in the Bailey Case, "that **a constitutional prohibition cannot be transgressed indirectly**

by the creation of a statutory presumption any more than it can be violated by direct enactment. The power to create presumptions is not a means of escape from constitutional restrictions." If a legislative body is without power to enact as a rule of evidence a statute denying a litigant the right to prove the facts of his case, certainly the power cannot be made to emerge by putting the enactment in the guise of a rule of substantive law. *Heiner v Donnan, 285 US 312 (1932)*

164) Note the <u>Handbook For Special Agents, Criminal Investigation Intelligence Division, Internal Revenue Service</u>.

(1) A presumption is a rule of law which **permits the drawing of a particular inference** as to the existence of the particular facts. Although it is **not evidence**, it may be considered as a **substitute for evidence**… (3) A **rebuttal presumption** is one which **prevails until it is overcome by evidence** to the contrary.

165) We must acknowledge that it is possible for federal agents to exceed their authority and to be held accountable.

Whatever the form in which the Government functions, anyone entering into an arrangement with the Government takes the risk of having accurately ascertained that he who purports to act for the Government stays within the bounds of his authority.

The scope of this authority may be explicitly defined by Congress or be limited by delegated legislation, properly exercised through the rule-making power. And this is even though, as here, **the agent himself may have been aware of the limitations upon his authority**. _Federal Crop Ins. Corp. v Merrill_, 332 US 380 (1947)

... the maxim that the King can do no wrong has no place in our system of government; yet it is also true, in respect to the State itself, that whatever wrong is attempted in its name is imputable to its government and not to the State, for, as it can speak and act only by law, whatever it does say and do must be lawful. **That which therefore is unlawful because made so by the supreme law, the Constitution of the United States is not the word or deed of the State, but is mere wrong and trespass of those persons who falsely spread and act in its name.** _Poindexter v Greenhow_, 114 US 270 (1885)

166) These citations confirm that an agent may be held accountable for failure to follow the law.

The officer may be sued only if he acts in excess of his statutory authority or in violation of the Constitution for then he ceases to represent the Government. _U.S ex. rel. Brookfield Const Co. v Stewart_, 284 F. Supp. 94 (1964)

No man in this country is so high that he is above the law. No officer of the law may set that law at defiance with impunity. All the officers of the government from the highest to the lowest, are creatures of the law and are bound to obey it. It is the only supreme power in our system of government. And every man who by accepting office participates in its functions is only the more strongly bound to submit to that supremacy, and to observe the limitations which it imposes upon the exercise of the authority which it gives. *United States v Lee, 106 US 196, 220 (1882)*

As expressed otherwise, the powers delegated to a public officer are held in trust for the people and are to be exercised in behalf of the government or of all citizens who may need the intervention of the officer. Furthermore, the view has been expressed that all public officers, within whatever branch and whatever level of government, and whatever be their private vocations, are trustees of the people, and accordingly labor under every disability and prohibition imposed by law upon trustees relative to the making of personal financial gain from a discharge of their trusts. That is, a public officer occupies a fiduciary relationship to the political entity on whose behalf he or she serves, and owes a fiduciary duty to the public. It has been said that the fiduciary responsibilities of a public officer cannot be less than those of a private individual. Furthermore, it has been stated that any enterprise undertaken by the public official which tends to weaken public confidence and undermine the sense of security for individual rights is against public policy. *63C American Jurisprudence2d, Public Officers and Employees, 247 (1999)*

167) Now, if the government makes a false presumption, may the Citizen, especially in a criminal trial, rebut that very presumption? One could easily argue that a false presumption made by an FBI agent, IRS Agent, BATF Agent, U.S. Attorney, or federal judge exceeds their authority and necessitates a rebuttal. Read below:

A presumption is neither evidence nor a substitute for evidence. Properly used, the term "presumption" is a rule of law directing that if a party proves certain facts (the "basic facts") at a trial or hearing, the factfinder [the judge or jury] must also accept an additional fact (the "presumed fact") as proven unless sufficient evidence is introduced tending to rebut the presumed fact. In a sense, therefore, a presumption is an inference which is mandatory unless rebutted. *American Jurisprudence 2d, Evidence 181* [brackets added]

168) The Internal Revenue Manual, Sec. 1132.75 limits the scope of criminal investigations.

The Criminal Investigation Branch enforces the criminal statute applicable to **income**, estate, gift, **employment** and excise tax laws... **involving United States citizens residing in foreign countries and nonresident aliens subject to federal income tax requirements.**

This text confirms the limited scope of the Internal Revenue Code to those *persons* or *individuals* subject to the tax.

169) The Supreme Court determined,

Congress has power to tax the income received by a **native citizen of the United States** domiciled abroad from property situated abroad. *Cook v Tait, 265 US 47, (1924)*

This decision is consistent with the Internal Revenue Manual.

170) Section 334.8 of the Handbook states the objectives of the BATF.

1) That the BATF is charged with enforcing **the tax laws on taxpayers as defined**, due to the illicit enterprises. 2) The BATF becomes an enforcement referral service for non-bureau violations and provides a list of names and addresses of **presumptive "taxpayers" for possible income** or wagering **tax investigations**.

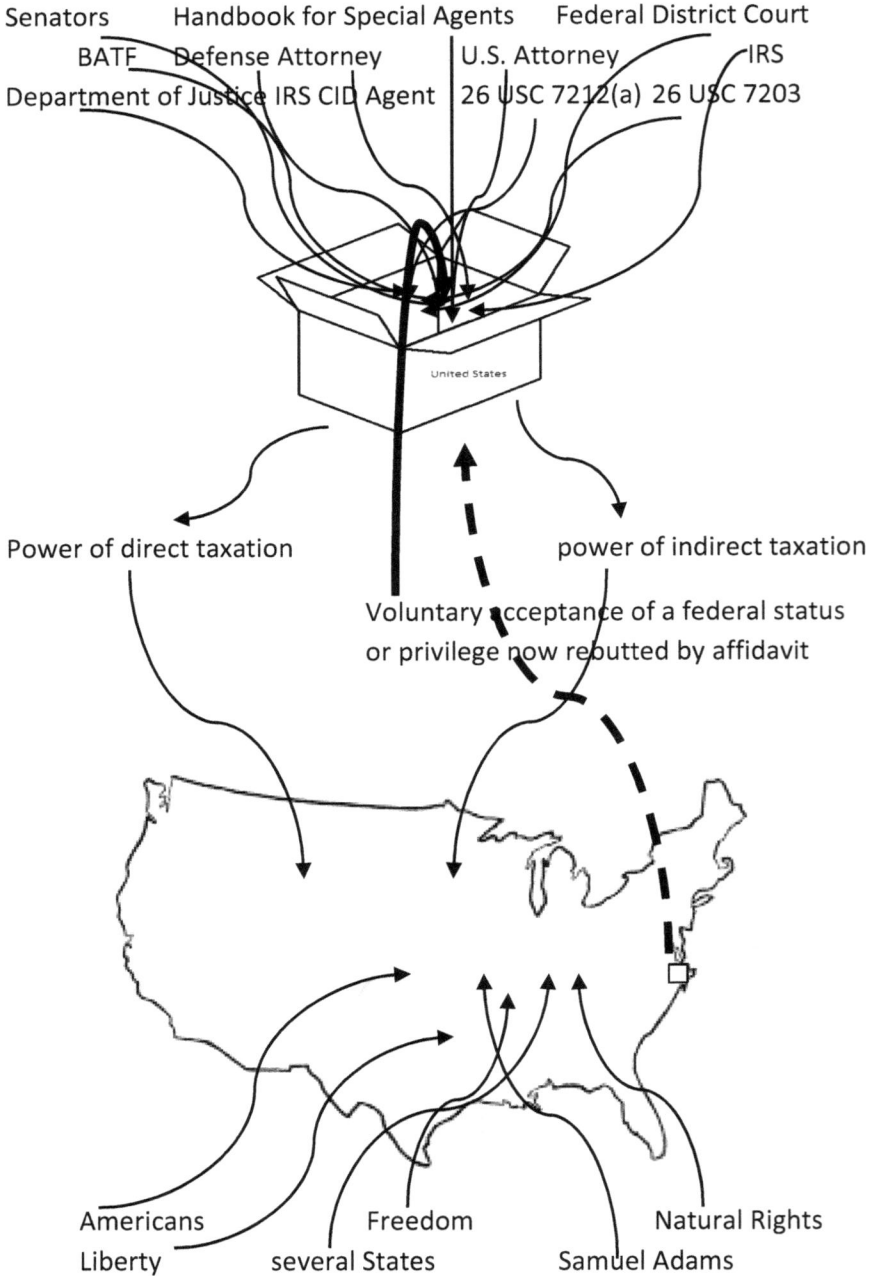

Senators   Handbook for Special Agents   Federal District Court

BATF   Defense Attorney   U.S. Attorney   IRS

Department of Justice IRS CID Agent   26 USC 7212(a) 26 USC 7203

United States

Power of direct taxation   power of indirect taxation

Voluntary acceptance of a federal status
or privilege now rebutted by affidavit

Americans   Freedom   Natural Rights

Liberty   several States   Samuel Adams

What is Taxable? What is Exempt?

171) The Internal Revenue Code, Subtitle A (the income tax law), limits liability for the imposition of a tax to partners (26 USC 701), foreign corporations (26 USC 884), and withholding agents liable for withholding taxes on *nonresident aliens* (26 USC 1461). The only other party liable for the income tax as stated in Subchapter C (employment taxes) is the *employer* (26 USC 3403). Now consider that under Subtitle A, Section 1 (26 USC 1), the tax is not imposed upon any *person*; it is imposed upon *taxable income*. Recall that titles are not law.

> 1. Tax on Individuals
> There is hereby imposed **upon the taxable income**...*26 USC 1*

172) Only those liable for the income tax are listed above. We know that not *every person* is liable. So, what is taxable? What is able to be taxed? The 16th Amendment states, "from whatever source derived." Knowing what "sources" are taxable is crucial, just as what is not taxable is vital to understand.

173) 26 USC 861 deals with "Income from **sources *within the United States.***"

> (a) Income from sources within the United States.
> The following items of gross income **shall be treated as income from sources within the United States**: *Subtitle A, Chapter 1 Normal Taxes and Surtaxes, Subchapter N Tax Based on Income from Sources within or without the United States, Part 1 Determination of Sources of Income, 26 USC 861*

While "items" are not "sources" and the term "sources" is not defined, the code refers to the regulations.

174) 26 CFR 1.861-8, Computation of taxable income from sources within the United States and from other sources and activities:

> (a) In general – (1) Scope. Sections 861(b) and 863(a) state in general terms how to determine taxable income of a taxpayer **from sources within the United States** after gross income from sources from within the United States has been determined. *Chapter 1 Internal Revenue Service, Department of the Treasury, Subchapter A Income Tax, Part 1 Income taxes Determination of Sources of Income*

We may conclude that some *sources* are taxable and some are not. Section 1.861-8 continues.

> ...The rules contained in this section apply in determining taxable income of the taxpayer from **specific sources and activities** under other sections of the Code, referred to in this section as operative sections. See paragraph (f)(1) of this section for a list and description of operative sections.

Section (f)(1) states:

> (f) Miscellaneous matters –
> (1) Operative sections. The operative sections of the Code which require the determination of taxable income of the taxpayer from specific sources or activities and which give rise to statutory groupings to which this section is applicable **include** the sections described below.

(i) Overall limitation to **the foreign tax credit**.

(ii) [Reserved]

(iii) **DISC and FSC** taxable income.

(iv) Effectively connected taxable income. **Nonresident alien individuals and foreign** corporations engaged in **trade or business within the United States**...

(v) **Foreign base company income**.

(vi) Other operative sections. The rules provided in this section also apply in determining –

(A) The amount of **foreign source items** of tax preference under section 58(g) determined for purposes of the minimum tax;

(B) The amount of **foreign mineral income** under section 901(e)

(C) [Reserved]

(D) The amount of foreign oil and gas extraction income and the amount of **foreign oil** related income under section 907;

(E) [Reserved]

(F) [Reserved]

(G) The limitation under section 934 on the maximum reduction of income tax liability **incurred in the Virgin Islands**;

(H) [Reserved]

(I) The special deduction granted **to China Trade Act corporations** under section 941;

(J) The amount of certain U.S. source income excluded from the subpart F income of a **controlled foreign corporation** under section 952(b);

(K) The amount of income from the **insurance of U.S. risks** under section 953(b)(5)

(L) The **international boycott factor** and the specifically attributable taxes and income under section 999; and (M)

The **taxable income** attributable to the operation of an agreement vessel under section 607 of the **Merchant Marine Act of 1936,** as amended, and the Capital Construction Fund Regulations thereunder (26 CFR, part 3). See 26 CFR 3.2(b)(3)

175) The listing of the "sources" and "activities" is important, as section 1.861-1 states,

> ... the expenses, losses and other deductions which **cannot definitely be allocated** to some item or class of gross income.

Curiously, but not surprisingly, the list of sources and activities under (f)(1) are foreign in nature. Moreover, we learn that deductions cannot be allocated to some classes.

176) But the question remains: Why isn't *all* income included in gross income? We need only refer to the tax code of 1939, which was based upon "net income," while the code of 1954 was based upon "gross income." The 1939 Code was consistent with the regulations, which stated,

> (b..) Exclusions from gross income. The following items **shall not be included in gross income and shall be exempt from taxation** under this chapter 19.22 (b)

177) Here we have certainty that some income is "exempt."

> 19.22(b) – 1 Exemptions – Exclusions from gross income. Certain items of income specified in section 22(b) **are exempt from tax** and may be excluded from gross income.

These items, however, are exempt only to the extent and in the amount specified. No other items are exempt from gross income **except** (1) **those items** of income which are, **under the Constitution, not taxable by the Federal Government**...

This revelation must be understood for what it is. The prior regulations defined gross income as virtually everything, yet acknowledged that, under constitutional law, some items are "not taxable by the Federal Government." This would be a confession in today's regulations. Did the 1939 regulations dignify that a man's earnings were not taxable?

178) The 1939 Code shows that not all income was taxed.

(F)(1) GENERAL RULE – A distribution made by a corporation to its shareholders in its stock or a right to acquire its stock shall not be treated as a dividend to the extent it **does not constitute income to the shareholder within the meaning of the Sixteenth Amendment to the Constitution.** 115(F)(1), 1939 Code

(2) if the distribution was not subject to tax in hands of such distributee because it **did not constitute income to him within the meaning of the Sixteenth Amendment to the Constitution**... *115(h)(2), 1939 Code*

With the 1954 code and regulations, reference to the *Constitution, Sixteenth Amendment, and fundamental law* were omitted. Such references were inconsequential since the tax was altered from *net income* in the 1939 Code to *taxable income*. The significance is that Congress could only tax income which was able to be taxed, as in taxable. Excluded or exempt income, by virtue of the Constitution, was unaffected regardless of the change. Yet, exempt or excluded income, which was inherently outside of congressional authority, was forgotten—out of sight, out of mind.

179) The current regulations hint of these past exclusions. The language under section 1.861-1 is written with the hint that not all income is taxable.

> (ii) Exempt income and assets defined –
> (A) In general. For purposes of this section, the term "exempt income" means any income that is in whole or part, **exempt, excluded or eliminated** for federal income tax purposes. *26 CFR 1-861-8T(d)(2)(ii) Computation of taxable income from sources within the United States and from other sources and activities.*

The language references the former wording of past codes and regulations which cited the constitutional prohibition of a tax.

180) The code then states what income is not tax exempt.

> (iii) **Income that is not considered tax exempt**.
> The following items are not considered to be tax exempt, eliminated, or excluded income and, thus, may have expenses, losses, or other deductions allocated and apportioned to them.
>
> (A) In the case of a **foreign taxpayer** (including a foreign sales corporation (FSC)) computing its effectively connected income, gross income (whether domestic or foreign source) which is not effectively connected to the conduct of a **United States trade or business**;

(B) In computing the combined taxable income of a DISC or FSC and its related supplier, the gross **income of a DISC or FSC**;

(C) For all purposes under subchapter N of the Code, including the computation of combined taxable income of a possessions corporation and its affiliates under section 936(h), **the gross income of a possession corporation** for which a credit is allowed under section 936(a); and

(D) **Foreign earned income** as defined in section 911 and the regulations thereunder (however, the rules of Sec. 1.911-6 do not require the allocation and apportionment of certain deductions, including home mortgage interest, to foreign earned income for purposes of determining the deductions disallowed under section 911(d)(6))

These four subsections *list* items which deal with foreign corporations, possessions corporations, and foreign earned income. Note, there is no reference to exempt items; yet, we know what is not exempt. We must conclude that income not listed as *not exempt* is *exempt*.

181) Congress acknowledges its limitations to tax—that there are items and sources which are exempt, as in not taxable by the Federal Government. We know, based upon the language of the current code, some income cannot be gross income, while the code and regulations identify sources which can be included in gross income when determining taxable income (1.861-8(f)(1)). The code and regulations state there is income which is exempt, while listing those items that are not exempt (1.861-8T(d)(2)(iii)).

182) In light of the foregoing, coupled with text and citations throughout this book, is there any doubt that Americans may seek to reclaim a status which was and is effectively exempt and excluded from federal taxation? Is there any doubt Americans may rebut the presumption and prima facie evidence that they are *taxpayers* and *U.S. persons* subject to the tax code? Is there any question they may seek to honor and live by the time-tested beliefs that a native citizen, an American, has natural rights which cannot be taken away or diminished? Do they not have the right to be left alone and to enjoy their prized freedom, while rejecting the perceived security which forsakes the spirit of self-reliance?

> The individual may stand upon his constitutional rights as a citizen. He is entitled to carry on his private business in his own way. His power to contract is unlimited. He owes no duty to the state or to his neighbors to divulge his business, or to open his doors to an investigation so far as it may tend to criminate him. He owes no such duty to the state, since he receives nothing therefrom, beyond the protection of his life and property. His rights are such as existed by the law of the land long antecedent to the organization of the state, and can only be taken from him by due process of law, and in accordance with the Constitution. *Hale v Henkel, 201 US 43, 74 (1906)*

26 USC 701 Partners 26 USC 884 Foreign Corporations 26 USC 3403
Employers   26 USC Subchapter A   26 USC 1 Taxable Income
1929 Code 19.22(b)-1   Exclusions from Gross Income   26 CFR
1.861-8 Taxable Income   IRS CID Agent   26 USC 1461
Withholding Agents 26 USC 861 Sources within the United States
     26 CFR 1.861-8T(d)(2)(ii) Income not exempt   26 USC 7203
     26 CFR 1.861-8(f)(1) Miscellaneous Matters   26 USC 7212(a)

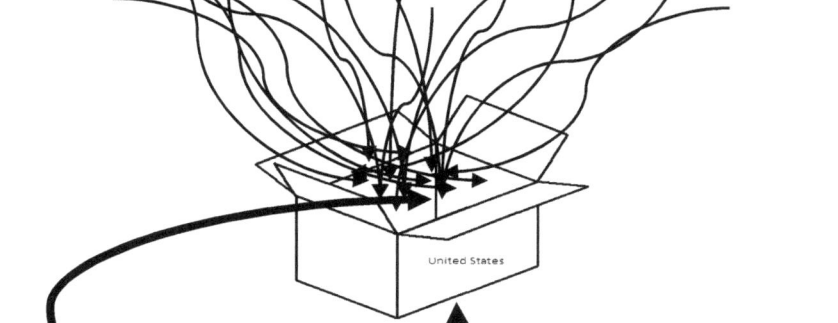

United States

Rebuttal of Presumption by Affidavit

Americans   Freedom   Natural Rights   Liberty
          Sovereign Citizens of the several States

Are You Within or Without

183) There are relevant questions: Are you included or excluded? Within or without? Dependent or independent? If we weigh the prima facie evidence and law, we may easily determine what and who is *within the United States*. If it includes Americans, the government has a presumption that we are liable.

184) Americans may decide they must rebut presumption of any liability for the income tax or that they are *U.S. persons*. Many may determine they no longer want to be classified with a federal status or dependent upon various federal benefits. By rebutting presumptions, one would be *without* the jurisdiction of the government.

> Clause 1. Subjects of jurisdiction.
> The judicial power shall extend to all Cases, in Law and Equity, arising under this Constitution, the Laws of the United States, and Treaties made, or which shall be made, under their Authority; - to all cases of admiralty and maritime jurisdiction; to **Controversies to which the United States shall be a Party**; to Controversies between two more States**; between a State and Citizens of another State**; **between Citizens of different States**, - between Citizens of the same State claiming lands under Grants of different States, **and between a State, or the Citizens thereof, and Foreign States, Citizens or Subjects**. *Article III Judicial Power, Section 2*

185) As is evident, the *class* of actions *within* the federal courts is limited. There are only three ways by which American Citizens may be brought within the subject matter jurisdiction of the

208

courts. Stated differently, there are only three ways the *United States* may acquire personam jurisdiction over the sovereign Citizens of the several States; otherwise, it is without jurisdiction.

a) One violates the "laws of the United States".
b) One is involved in a controversy "to which the United States shall be a party."
c) As a Citizen of a State, one is in a controversy with another "State."

186) If Americans knowingly or unknowingly create the presumption that they are *within the United States* for the purpose of the income tax code, they must rebut that very presumption. With such rebuttals, would Americans be within the jurisdiction of the federal courts as U.S. persons with the obligation to answer criminal charges for "failure to file an income tax return?" If Americans are not or never were within the taxing power of the *United States*, the Government would be without jurisdiction to seek an indictment. How could the federal government proceed with a legal action against one who rejects or never accepts a federal status or benefit? How could the government establish grounds to indict those who rebut the prima facie evidence and presumption that they are within the jurisdiction of congressional indirect taxing power, unless by either a proper counter of that rebuttal or by deceit and force?

187) The United States presumes authority and jurisdiction without question. Regardless of the controversy, unwitting and ignorant Americans typically conclude that jurisdiction is acquired by the government merely because it asserts the same. This is no different than an American gratuitously and thoughtlessly concluding that the legal term *United States* means the 50 States.

Consider how and why the *United States* brings criminal charges against Americans.

188) In a federal tax trial, while many believe the victim is the *United States* or the *United States of America*, the actual victim is the Internal Revenue Service. In the government's case, the IRS, the very agency which conducts the criminal investigation (which is suspect), is listed as the victim in the Pre-Sentence Investigation Report. Why isn't the IRS listed as the Plaintiff? The answer may rest in part with the definition of "agency."

189) Under 18 USC, which deals with crimes,

> The term "agency" includes any department, independent establishment, commission, administration, authority, board or bureau of the United States or any corporation in which the United States has a proprietary interest... *Section 6, Department and Agency Defined.*

190) In the "historical" section of 18 USC 1001, we learn that the

> Words "or any corporation in which the United States of America is a stockholder" in said section 80 were omitted as unnecessary in view of "agency" in section 6 of this title. *Chapter 47 Fraud and False Statements, Historical; Ancillary Law and Directives.*

However, the code still contains language stating "corporation in which the United States has a proprietary interest." Is the "United States of America" the same as the "United States?" Under "History; Ancillary Laws and Directives" of section 6, we learn:

The phrase "corporation in which the United States has a proprietary interest" is intended to include those government corporations in which stock is not actually issued, as well as those in which stock is owned by the United States.

191) From the definition of the term *agency*, is the IRS a "department, independent establishment, commission, administration, authority, board or bureau of the United States?" Is it a "corporation in which the United States has a proprietary interest?" If so, it would stand to reason the *United States*, under Article III, Section 2, Clause 1 would have grounds to file suit on behalf of the IRS as an *agency* in which the government has a proprietary interest.

192) Let's refute the three possible ways the *United States* could bring suit within the federal courts. First, if one rebutted the presumption that he was liable for a federal income tax, if only because the *United States* presumed he had a federal status or received a federal benefit, there would be no violation of "the laws of the United States." Second, as a Citizen of the several States, as one without the *United States*, he would no longer have a controversy with the *State* that is the *United States* or any of its territories or possessions. Finally, although the *United States* may be a party to any suit which involves the IRS, one would be without any binding nexus or contractual obligation with either the IRS or *United States* and, therefore, not involved with any controversy.

193) The federal income tax is legal and lawful, authorized by the indirect taxing power of Congress, enforced by the executive branch, and upheld by the federal courts. We must acknowledge

the legitimacy of any indirect tax, those subject to the tax, how they become liable, and how to overcome that presumed liability. *U.S. persons, persons and individuals*, as defined in the tax code, voluntarily obligate themselves for the tax. Their decision to engage in a taxable status or activity, even without fully informed consent, creates the obligation.

194) One may rebut that he is a *taxpayer* within the *United States* by rebutting the prima facie evidence and presumption.

195) Are you included or excluded, within or without? Are you dependent or independent? These queries are essential when one applies the law. Congressional powers are limited by design and necessity. The Supreme Court, not long before the influence of Justice Cardozo and jurists of his ilk, expressed reservations for failing to adhere to the Constitution.

> It will be an evil day for American Liberty **if the theory of a government outside supreme law of the land finds lodgment in our constitutional jurisprudence**. No higher duty rests upon this Court than to exert its full authority to **prevent all violations** of the principles of the Constitution. *Downes v Bidwell*, 182 US 244, 382 (1901)

196) Ten years before the 1894 Income Tax Act, the Court said,

> It may be that it is the obnoxious thing in its mildest and least repulsive form; but **illegitimate and unconstitutional practices get their first footing** in that way; namely, **by silent approaches and slight deviations from legal modes of procedure**. This can only be obviated by adhering to the rule that **constitutional provisions for the security of persons**

and property should be liberally construed. A close and literal construction deprives them of half their efficacy, and leads to gradual depreciation of the right, as if it consisted more in sound than in substance. **It is the duty of the Courts to be watchful for the Constitutional Rights of the Citizens**, and against any stealthy encroachments thereon. Their motto should be Obsta Principiis. We have no doubt that the legislative body is actuated by the same motives; but the vast accumulation of public business brought before it sometimes prevents it, on first impression, from noticing objections which become developed by time and the practical application of the objectionable law. *Boyd v United States*, *116 US 616, 635 (1885)*

197) As to the exercise of judicial jurisdiction, the Court said,

We have no more right to decline the exercise of jurisdiction which is given, than to usurp that which is not given. The one or the other would be treason to the Constitution. *Cohen v Virginia*, *6 Wheat 264, 404 (1821)*

198) The following diagram depicts the United States. The United States, as defined in 26 USC 7701, includes the District of Columbia, Puerto Rico, the Virgin Islands, and Guam. We already determined the several States would be included when any of them elected to participate under any particular federal authority, or when obligated to a delegated federal power under the Constitution. Consequently, the States which committed to the federal Social Security scheme would be *within the United States*. Does acceptance by the 50 States include the sovereign Citizens, which is a distinction acknowledged by the Supreme Court? While the answer was given before, this diagram underscores it.

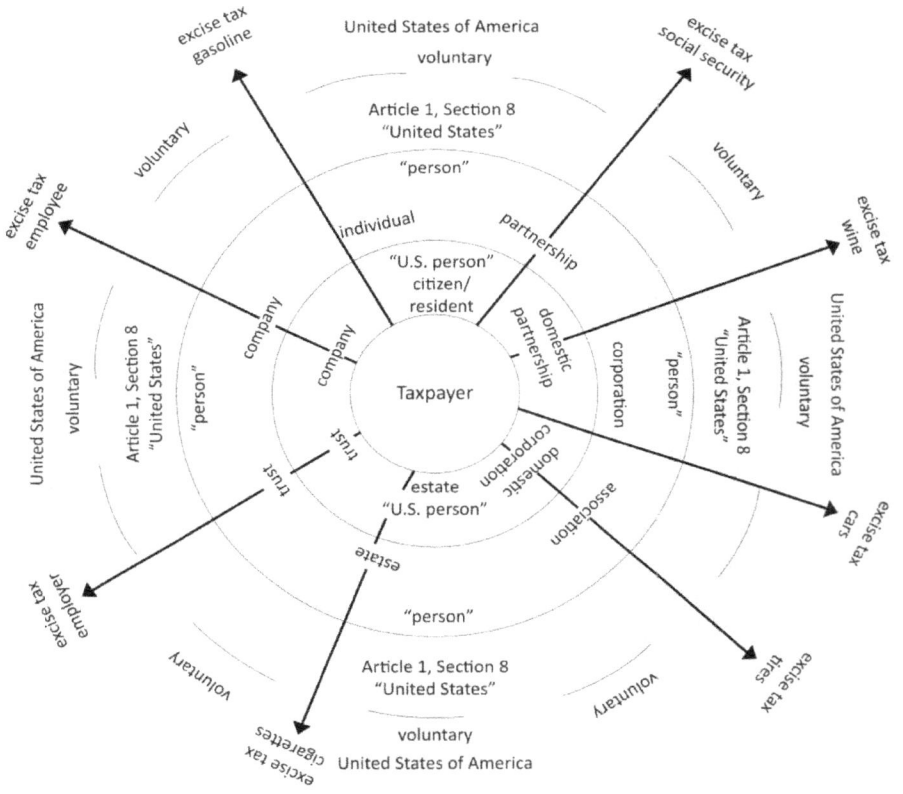

199) The second inner circle from the center represents those entities within the definition of *person* under 26 USC 7701(1). Are you any of these? The first circle from the center represents those entities within the definition of *United States person*, 26 USC 7701(30). Is this you? These entities, designated or classified as such by the Federal Government, are liable for the tax.

200) Under Article 1, Section 8 of the Constitution, the *United States* may tax all people within its power. Americans who voluntarily choose to buy cigarettes or gasoline, or accept a federal status/privilege, are liable for the corresponding excise.

> Term "revenue law" when used in connection with jurisdiction of courts of United States means law imposing duties or tonnage, or law providing in terms of revenue; **law must be directly traceable to power granted to Congress by [Section] 8, Article 1 of the Constitution,** "to lay and collect taxes, imposts and excises." *United States v Hill, 123 US 681 (1887)*

The foregoing quote is found in Title 28, section 1340 (Part IV Jurisdiction and Venue, Chapter 85 District Courts; jurisdiction, 1340. Internal Revenue; customs duties, Case Notations, II Internal revenue, 6. Generally.) We cannot escape the legal distinction of the term "revenue law" as it relates to the jurisdiction of the courts.

> Term **"revenue law"** when used **in connection with federal jurisdiction** means law which was clearly traceable to power granted to congress by [Section] 8 of Article 1 of the Constitution of United States to lay and collect taxes, duties, imposts and excises. *California ex rel. McColgan v Bruce*

(1942 CA9) Nev) 129 F. 2d 421, 147 ALR 782 cert den (1942) 317 US 678, 87 L Ed 544, 63 S Ct 157 reh den (1942) 317 US 710, 87 L Ed 566, 63 S Ct 255 [brackets added]

201) Are you within or without, included or excluded? If we desire to live within freedom and without the *United States*, Americans must rebut a presumption of federal jurisdiction created voluntarily, even if done so unknowingly. Americans have God-given natural rights. The *United States* Government has constitutional constraints. The distinction between the two is apparent. We need only take possession of the truth and the hope which springs from its essence.

202) Consider the following:

20 CFR Employee's Benefits
404.1905 termination of agreements
Each **agreement shall contain provisions for its possible termination**. If an agreement is terminated, entitlement to benefits and coverage acquired by an individual before termination shall be retained. The agreement shall provide for notification of termination to the other party and the effective date of termination.

In common usage, the term "person" does not include the sovereign, and statutes employing the word are ordinarily construed to exclude it. *Wilson v Omaha Indian tribe*, 442 US 653, 667 (1979)

203) The following example underscores the significance of the overall message within <u>The Rebutted Presumption</u>. The plaintiff filed an action for a declaratory judgment that he was not a

216

taxpayer. Yet, the Court could not do so. Why? If Rowen had an obligation to the income tax as a *person, United States person,* or any moniker within the subject class, couldn't the judge stipulate to this fact? No. The court did not have jurisdiction.

> Specifically, Rowen seeks a declaratory judgment against the United States of America with respect to "whether or not the plaintiff is a taxpayer pursuant to, and/or under 26 U.S.C. 7701(a)(14). The Court lacks jurisdiction to issue a declaratory judgment "with respect to Federal taxes other than actions brought under section 748 of the Internal Revenue Code of 1986," a code section that is not at issue in the instant action. See 28 U.S.C. 2201; see also Hughes v United States, 953 F.2d 531, 536-537 (9th Cir. 1991) (affirming dismissal of claim for declaratory relief under 2201 where claim concerned question of tax liability.) *Rowen v United States, 05-3766MMC (N.D. Cal. 11/02/2005)*

Solutions

1)   The *United States* tax code is constitutional. With respect to income taxes, the tax code is limited to *income* effectively connected to a federal status and privilege. The IRS has a responsibility to collect taxes on *income* directly attributable to *wages* in the performance of a *trade or business*, otherwise known as a *public office*. Since the jurisdiction of the federal government is constrained by the Constitution, the tax code is limited in scope as well. The misapplication or incorrect enforcement of the code against informed Americans who know they are not *U.S. persons* with a liability is regrettable.

2)   The Cardozo decisions are the interpretation of a few men. Their decisions facilitated the ceding of more freedom. Since the 1930s, we have lost a grounded context that Americans could not be within the *United States* for an indirect excise that must be voluntary, at least initially, before the *United States* may presume a continued liability.

3)   Prior to the 1930s, people understood they were not liable. Americans who operated privately were not within congressional power for this exaction. Yet, if only because Americans submitted federal forms and confirmed the incumbent federal nexus, they became *taxpayers*. Americans are subject to this excise until they correct the mistake.

4)   Some Americans have researched the tax laws and confirmed the obligation of taxpayers and the lack of any liability of non taxpayers. They have perfected the submission of forms to receive a return of funds paid for Social Security—an excise tax. It

should be transparent that a rebuttal of the presumption obviates any federal status and receipt of a privilege.

5)   Under 26 USC 6013(g)(4)(h), informed Americans hold the IRS accountable for the proper classification of their correct status. The IRS complies with the law and makes the necessary corrections. Does the IRS challenge such submissions? Yes. Some may receive a "frivolous filing" letter, which may likely induce the fear which causes the requestor to comply with the government's presumption. However, it is undeniable that the government will follow the law; for, it can do no differently in the end.

6)   The Rebutted Presumption reveals that we are unknowingly led to the erroneous conclusion of our liability for federal excise and income taxes, just as we were once without the obligation. The *United States* may only tax those within its domain. Now that we know our dilemma, that we have placed ourselves *within the United States* by accepting a federal status or benefits, we must effectively rebut this presumption.

7)   The following solutions serve the purpose of either preventing Americans from entering or extracting themselves from the matrix that is the federal domain and income tax system. We know by now the government may only tax who and what is within its power and it may not directly tax Americans.

8)   The sooner we understand this concept, the better. As it stands, the tax code has served as a means of control. The Federal Government has a direct accounting of not only what is earned, but what we do with our lives to the minutest detail.

Consider the following illustration. There is a federal building in Texas which has a secure climate-controlled room on the top floor with a computer. With strokes of the keyboard, the computer reveals an exhaustive history associated with any social security or tax identification number. The number you use, which belongs to the government, is a means of tracking Americans. The details in this history are more than we can imagine.

9)   The name associated with the Social Security number is the mirror image of our names, a double, a twin, a parallel persona within the federal matrix. The only difference is that the name is in all CAPITAL letters. The *United States* concludes that the CAPITAL name, a distinct legal *entity*, is you! You serve as Trustee for this government entity, an entity it created. This is the means by which the *United States* exercises control of an unsuspecting people. The correlation of these NAMES to our beings within a massive database began with a presumption we created.

10) Solutions:

A)   Research how to properly rebut your status as a *taxpayer* on any and all appropriate government forms; for most or all forms further the presumption. For example, most Americans submitted an SS-5 form to receive a Social Security Number. One would need to use another SS-5 to correct this mistake and change the language where appropriate. Why? Although it states otherwise, the Social Security Administration (SSA) does not provide a form for the purpose of revoking or rescinding the SSN.

Candidly, the Federal Government is not going to provide a form for people to exit the system with ease. As such, one must refute the information mistakenly entered in the past and establish a status as other than federal. Do this without a financial motive. If the aim is consistent with the law, any refund should follow.

B)   File an affidavit with the Social Security Administration and the Department of Internal Revenue which rebuts the government's presumption. This is essential. The government operates upon the initial submission of tax forms which place us within a *class* within its authority. Federal officials gladly assert power over an unaware people who become what they never knew could be prevented. Use the affidavit as a defense in any proceeding, especially for criminal charges in court. Your affidavit is the document you want the jury to read.

C)   Research filing a "final return" with the IRS.

D)   Correct mistakes made with your *employer* and federal *employment* tax forms.

E)   Take steps to protect your family. Terminate your relationship with the Social Security Administration. If we prudently plan for our retirement, we would not need this flawed and now defunct federal ponzi scheme. Such is the irony of Justice Cardozo. He espoused a *living law* to accommodate for a *social justice* of his own crafting. We are left with the ravages of his inferior thinking. A free people are free to the extent that they are not dependent.

F)   Do not secure a birth certificate or Social Security number for your newborn children. Hospitals will tell you this is required by law. What may be true is that hospitals must comply and complete certain information. A hospital's legal obligations do not concern you and your child. Informed Americans document the birth of their own children. You have every reason to document events such as births, marriages, and deaths in your family Bible, one means of recording events. When they are of legal age, allow your children to make their own decisions as to whether or not they request a Social Security number.

G)   There is no doubt that we live in a federally-focused system. The several States have become agents of a massive federal construct. Research the significance of what Justice Jackson referred to as the "administrative state."[22] We must elect representatives who will honor and comply with Article 1, Section 8 of the Constitution and restrain the influence of the government.

H)   As the electorate, we should exercise control. We should resist any suggestion of a tax that is inconsistent with the limits of congressional authority.

I)   We should learn from the past, which would enable us to better understand our present and future. If we understood the topics of finance and banking, we would understand the purpose of the income tax. Whether taxes pay interest to the owners of the Federal Reserve Bank, which is a privately held corporation and not at all federal, or to stave off inflation by siphoning money out of the economy, such insight is profitable. Read The Creature From

---

[22]

http://scholarship.law.cornell.edu/cgi/viewcontent.cgi?article=2539&context=clr

Jekyll Island by Edward Griffin. This is an excellent book about the creation of the Federal Reserve Bank. The Whiskey Rebellion by William Hogeland, describes America's fight against the first excise tax. Hogeland also explains a perspective on the role of finance and banking that is infrequently discussed.

The world is controlled by powerful banking families and central banks. The objectives of these institutions may appear sincere, but there is an agenda for control and profit. However, as explained in Debt Virus, two countries operate without a debt-based currency. Change is possible. May we realize a secure future is possible with a currency that serves the interests of the people and not the greed of those who control a global system.

America was once a world financial power with no debt. We are now the world's largest debtor nation. We have huge budgets and catastrophic deficits, with no means to satisfy our obligations.

There is a direct correlation between our lack of financial discipline and the relinquishing of our natural rights. We have ceded our rights to labor (property) for federal classifications and benefits which culminate in greater federal control. Our deliberate intent to reverse this dynamic would enhance our freedom. If we coveted our rights, if we prized private property as paramount, if we retained what is ours alone, the abundance that would naturally ensue would be without parallel. Imagine millions of Americans with their entire earnings at their disposal. The influx of dollars injected into the economy would be unprecedented. The resulting collection of proper excise taxes would correspond with America's subsequent prosperity.

26 USC 701 Partners 26 USC 884 Foreign Corporations 26 USC 3403
FBI Employers DOJ C A trade or business forts and arsenals Article 1
Section 8 American Employer MRS MORSE 26 USC 1 Tax regulations
26 USC Subchapter A USC 1 Taxable Income Guam direct taxes 1929
Code 19.22(b)-1 Article 1, Section 2 nonresident alien individuals
Puerto Rico District of Columbia Virgin Islands YOU Exclusions from
Gross Income 26 CFR 1.861-8 Taxable Income EIN, SSN TIN Senators
Representatives 26 USC 1461 Withholding Agents 26 USC 861 US
Army Sources within the United States 26 CFR 1.861-8T(d)(2)(iii) US
Navy BATF US Air Force NSA 5 USC US employees FICA federal
courts 42 USC individuals aliens IRS 26 CFR MR BURNS YOU
Income not exempt 26 CFR 1.861-8(f)(1) Miscellaneous Matters IRS
CID Agent 16th Amendment Constitution US persons W-2 forms
26 USC 7212(a) IRS Social Security Wages 26 USC 7203 Sources of
Income 26 USC 861 Employment Taxes

PRESUMPTION CREATED   **PRIMA FACIE EVIDENCE**

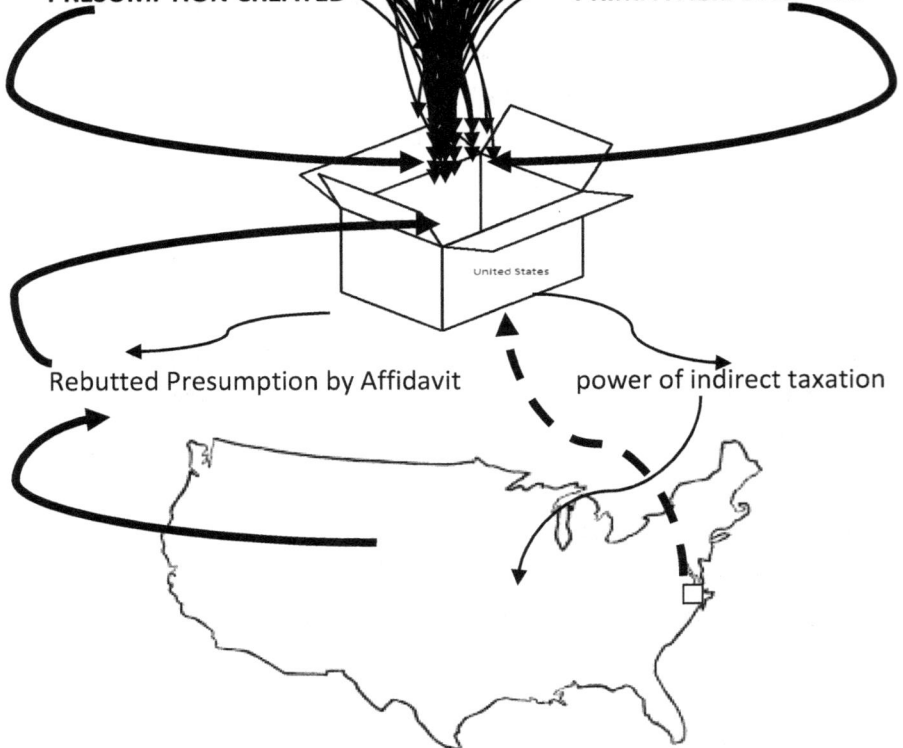

Rebutted Presumption by Affidavit   power of indirect taxation

224

Conclusion

Referring to the *within* and *without* concept, consider a 6th grade level review as to how and why Americans are exempt from and *U.S. persons* are liable for federal excise and income taxes.

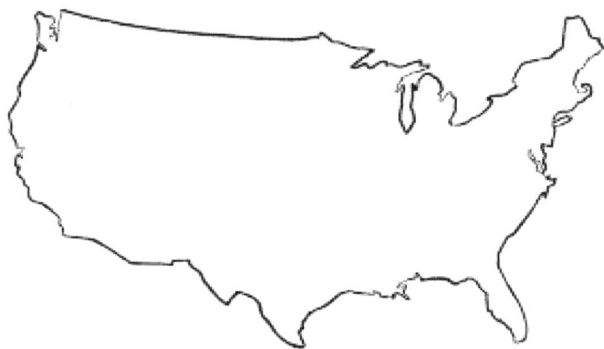

This is the united States of America–the 50 States of the Union.

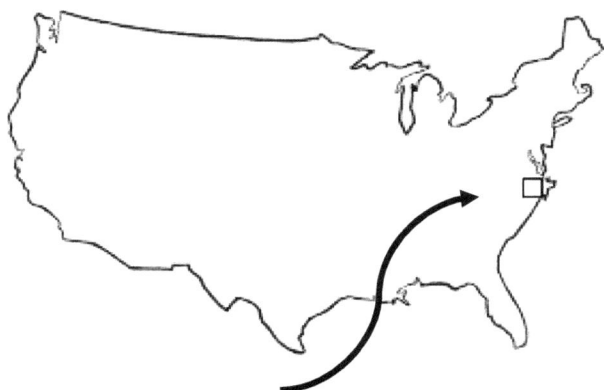

This is the *United States*—a federal territory.

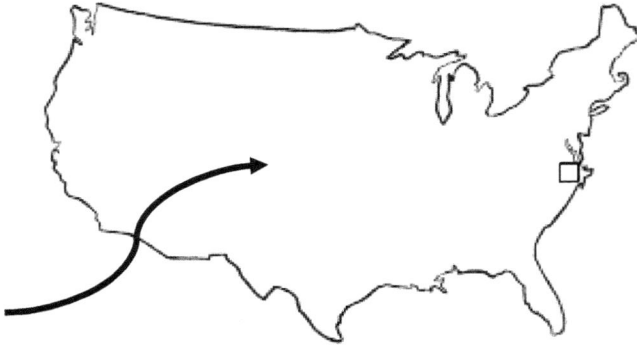

Within the 50 States, Americans enjoy life, liberty, and property.

Labor and Earnings

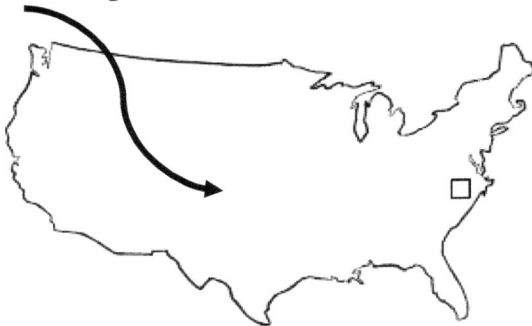

Americans work. Their labor and earnings are property.

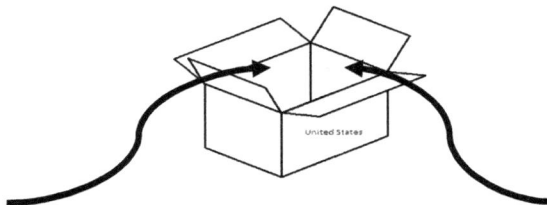

The United States has control over Territories, Possessions, District of Columbia and powers under Article 1, Section 8

United States   America

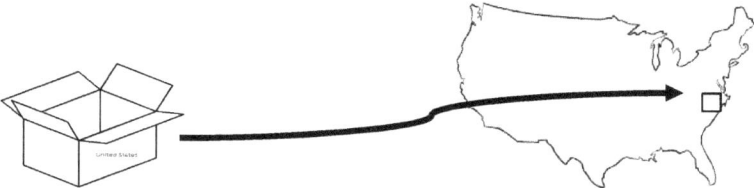

The *United States* is a distinct entity seated in Washington, D.C. with limited jurisdiction and power within the 50 States.

United States   America

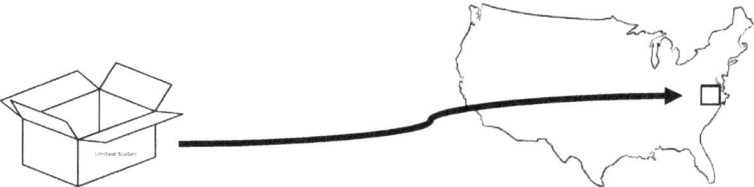

Congress may directly tax Americans or their property by apportionment only.

United States   America

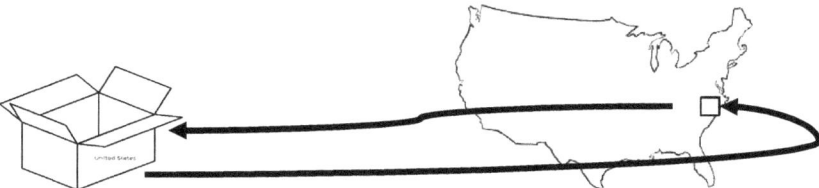

Congress may indirectly tax those who voluntarily engage a federal taxable activity, privilege, or benefit.

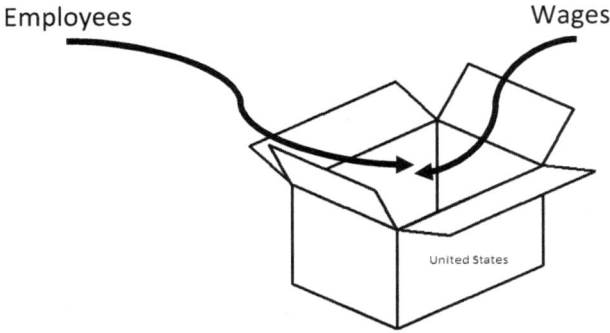

With the Social Security Act of 1935, Congress created a federal benefit which indirectly taxes the *wages* of all *employees* within the jurisdiction of the *United States*.

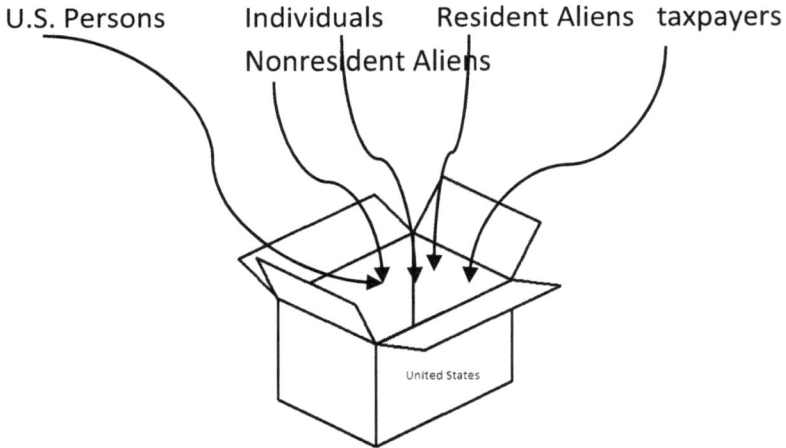

The tax code defines those liable for the federal income tax by legal terms: *employees, persons, individuals, U.S. persons, resident aliens, nonresident aliens, and taxpayers*.

Social Security

Freedom

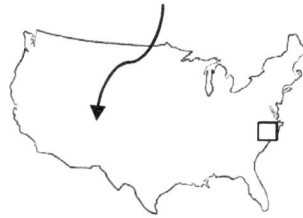

United States

America

Americans are not required to accept Social Security.

Social Security

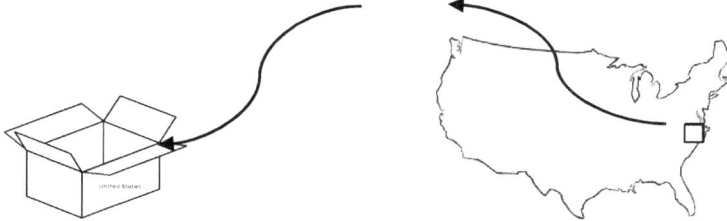

United States

America

Those who accept Social Security are *within the United States.*

Americans are free
within the 50 States

U.S. persons are federal and
within the United States

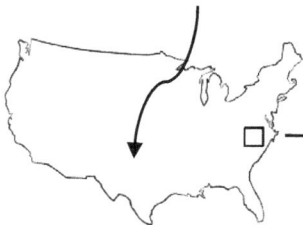

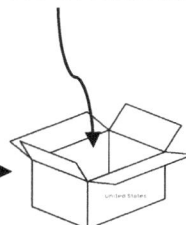

U.S. persons are under federal control and file tax forms.

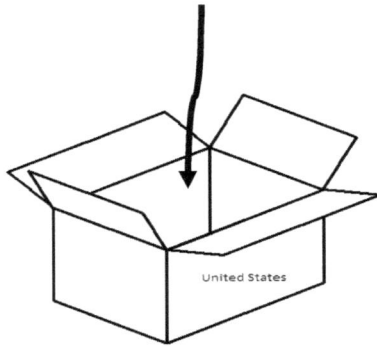

U.S. persons

United States

The *United States* presumes *U.S. persons* are within its jurisdiction.

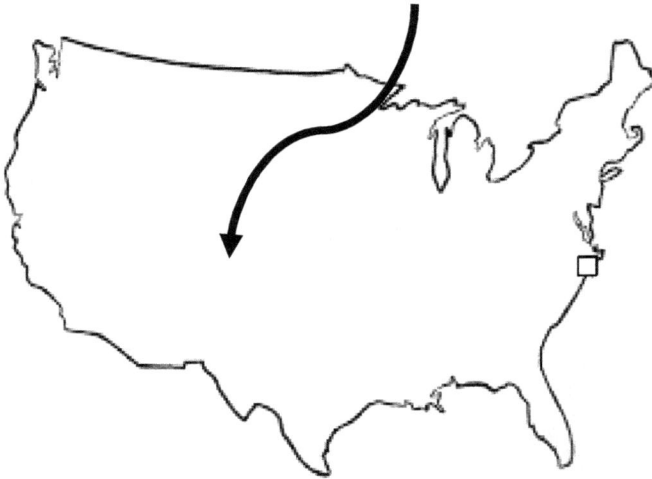

Americans

The government does not exercise jurisdiction over sovereign Citizens within the several States.

U.S. persons file tax returns
W-4, 1040 Forms

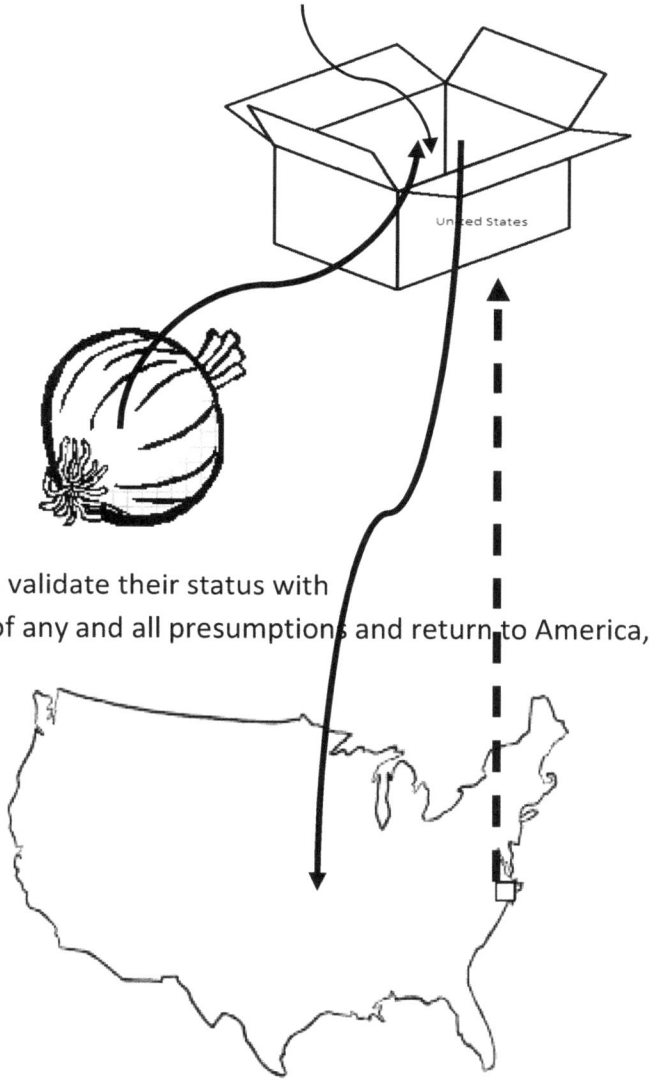

Americans validate their status with
rebuttals of any and all presumptions and return to America,

the land of the free and the home of the brave.

Final Exam

Would you prefer to be **within** the United States

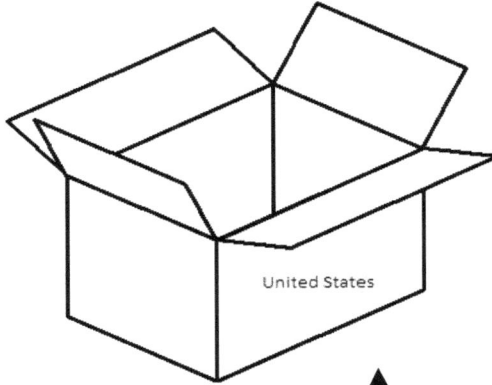

United States

Or **within** the

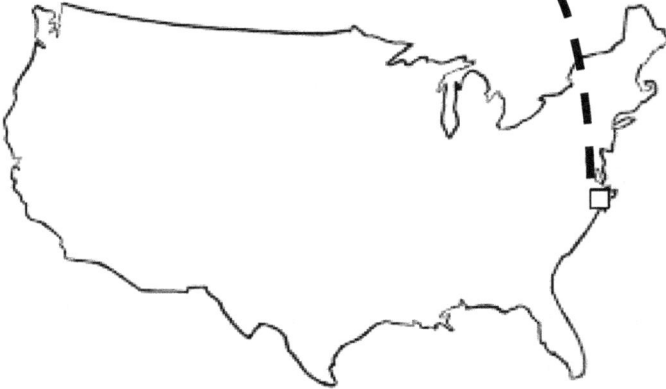

the several States of the united States of America?

Epilogue

In November 2016, I mailed a certified letter to the Social Security Administration, signed under penalty of perjury, in which I resigned as compelled Social Security trustee. Although I had effectively done the same in 2000, given my experience at the hands of the corrupt justice system, I chose to memorialize this decision and with such measures that would ensure the document was admissible in a court of law. Just before publishing The Rebutted Presumption, the Social Security Administration sent a reply.

Let's reaffirm some fundamentals as we review the SSA's language. The *Federal Government* cannot have *jurisdiction* over those who are not within its purview. The United States is a *corporation, a legal fiction* that exists within Washington, D.C. and exercises only those powers delegated to it by the people under Article 1, Section 8 of the Constitution. The Social Security Administration (SSA) is a federal *agency* with limited powers to satisfy the requirements of the *federal statute* under 42 USC and the regulations under 20 CFR. Those within the jurisdiction or *employees* in a *trade or business* on behalf of the *United States* are obligated to comply, voluntarily, with SSA mandates. Since we have a solid understanding of the legal terms which govern the law and courts, we are more aware of jurisdictional issues and the limited scope of federal authority.

We should readily appreciate the language the SSA used in its response. Noteworthy, the SSA letter is without a signature and is not signed under penalty of perjury or with any attestation to the truth of the matter by an agent of the agency. This is a classic form letter, a template behind which the SSA hides. Federal agencies use the prestige of the government without an officer or federal agent accountable for his decisions or actions.

Sadly, most Americans would accept this SSA response as valid—as law. Americans would not rebut such conclusions. This is the desired effect of the deceit of the United States. The Government cannot risk thousands of educated Americans, who are not within or employed by the *United States*, resigning as trustees to legal fictions—*government entities*.

The SSA letter begins with "People cannot voluntarily end their participation in the program." Is this true? Perhaps it is for those obligated under the legal codes. Does this statement affect those who are not within the orbit of SSA powers in the first place? No. The SSA then offers, "Unless specifically *exempt* by law, *everyone* working in the *United States must* pay Social Security *taxes*." If we consider the words in italics, we see legal terms reflected in the content of this book. Yes, this statement is true for *everyone* working in the *United States,* as they *must* pay *taxes* unless *exempt*. Since the SSA *presumes* that I am such a *person* and ignores my *rebuttal* of its presumption, the agency refuses to acknowledge the truth——I am without its authority.

The SSA then states, "A *person must voluntarily file* an application to receive Social Security *benefits*." Is this statement not true for those *within* the authority of the *United States*? We must recall that a benefit is accepted voluntarily. Moreover, this is an excise, an indirect tax, which must be paid as a result accepting the benefit. This is vital to understand. Otherwise, the federal government does not have the wherewithal to *force* Americans to *voluntarily* accept any benefit. Next, the agency says, "Once you have a Social Security number, we cannot cancel or destroy the record." I do not object to the SSA stating what *it* cannot do, whether true or not. I am concerned about my responsibilities under the law and the SSA's attendant liabilities.

The SSA underscores its position with, "The Supreme Court has upheld the constitutionality of the Social Security Act." Based upon our research in this book, we must agree. The Court has confirmed that *the Act*—a federal statute—is a legitimate power that is enforceable within the constraints of congressional taxing authority. What does the exercise of a legitimate constitutional power have to do with an American living in freedom within the several States and one who is without congressional taxing jurisdiction?

Finally, as if the foregoing discussion is not enough proof concerning the limits of federal authority, the SSA states, "The United States Citizenship and Immigration Services has *jurisdiction* over the issue of *citizenship*. Please direct any questions you may have about citizenship to the U.S. Citizenship and Immigration Services..." Let's simplify this observation. If an American is born within one of the 50 States of the Union, is he not a Citizen of that State and, thus, a Citizen of the **united** States of America? The *United States* Government has a constitutional responsibility to oversee immigration and to grant a legal status to those entering the *United States*. It has no authority over the Citizenship of the sovereign people born within the 50 States. The United States does not grant or deny Citizenship to those born in America. We already established that the Supreme Court held that one could be a Citizen of the several States, but not be a *citizen of the United States*. The *United States* may have citizens of its own, while the 50 States have distinct Citizens.

We must concede that Americans who enter the *United States* for a benefit are *within* the jurisdiction of the *United States*. This is beyond dispute. The *United States* has plenary power within its jurisdiction and grants citizenship to those within its domain. We need only recognize the efforts of President Trump as he attempts to deny terrorists any access to the United

States—those who do not have Citizenship or *permission* to enter America. Meanwhile, the government cannot deny entry or exit to those who have a legal status, whether by Green Card, Visa, or citizenship. Weigh this question: Is the federal government able to affect the reasonable ingress or egress of Americans to the land to which they belong by birthright?

The SSA letter should give us pause and reason to ponder the implications of unchecked federal authority. The more *power*, especially unlawful and unconstitutional power, that Americans shamelessly concede to the *United States*, the less free they are. If we consider the Affordable Care Act (federal statute), known as Obama Care, we see the devastating impact of what I refer to as "Federal Creep." When the government gains greater power by an incremental and often undetected creeping over time, the government acquires what was impossible and inconceivable. Ironically, what was once unthinkable eventually becomes possible, all a result of our collective ignorance.

To understand the essence of the authority that precipitated the ability of the *United States* Government to control the entire healthcare system, we must reconsider the question of jurisdiction. If we were to read the Supreme Court decision written by Chief Justice John Roberts,[23] we would learn one salient point. The Supreme Court defines those liable to Obama Care as *taxpayers*. Yes, the *United States* is merely exercising authority, narrowly defined, to those already within its scope. Congress may regulate and control by congressional legislation those who are within its domain. Naturally, Congress requires *U.S. persons* already within its control to participate in a federal power Congress may only exercise within the *United States*. Are you able

---

[23] https://www.supremecourt.gov/opinions/11pdf/11-393c3a2.pdf

to deny what Roberts and the Supreme Court narrowly articulated in writing?

Who is responsible for assessing and collecting the fines or penalties associated with a *U.S. person's* failure to subscribe to Obama Care? *It is the Internal Revenue Service*. Are you a taxpayer or a non taxpayer? Have you even considered how and why the *United States* Congress has power to legislate the particulars of America's healthcare system? Are you liable to anything and everything Congress dictates by legislation simply because you are pigeon-holed into a class of *persons* beholden to the Federal Government with and through the IRS?

Are you free?

Letter to the American People

<u>The Rebutted Presumption</u> began with a graph depicting the amount of spending by the *United States* Government. It may be obvious by now that funds from the Social Security Act is a main source for this reckless situation. Funds for the supposed safety and security of *United States persons*, funds that are not secured within a trust account within the Department of the Treasury, allow elected representatives to further unwarranted reach and control of the federal government into every facet of American life.

What was once unknown, nuanced, and confused becomes clear. The federal government fosters the notion you are legally obligated to the *income* tax and the excise upon *wages* as an *employee*. It should be evident you have this liability as a *person* within the jurisdiction of the *United States*. Moreover, it should be clear you do not have to accept a federal status or privilege that binds you to these excises.

With a proper understanding of legal language in the income tax code and regulations reflected as a graph, we would have a rising line running parallel with increased autonomy of Americans. The power of the federal government and its capacity to collect funds would be reflected by descending lines.

Now, consider the next thought carefully. If the government had to protect its undue influence over a free people, who would otherwise be *without* its jurisdiction, it would, at all costs, deny any rebuttals of presumption of a tax liability. How is this possible in a country that prizes justice and truth under the law? How does the government demand that the willing and uninformed comply with the income tax laws? By and through deception, deflection, and subterfuge, and if needed, raw force.

Consider a striking contrast. I am a Distinguished Military Graduate from the Virginia Military Institute. With a top-secret clearance, I served honorably as an Army officer and Company Commander in the Military Intelligence field. I am now a *convicted felon* who served a federal prison sentence for purportedly violating federal income tax laws. I am innocent and I am not unaware. I know the truth. I also understand procedures used for covert operations and that government ploys are predicated upon deceit. Once a cover is established with available assets, officials deflect and ignore attempts to disclose the truth. In the intelligence world, deceit is achieved by disinformation, subterfuge, and denial.

Americans are subject to government deceit within the federal income tax system. If you write to elected officials for the law which requires an American to file a federal income tax return, they will not reply with a specific response. Rather, they will forward your letter to the IRS. The IRS will issue a boilerplate answer that will be inadequate at best. The IRS will then send its letter to your representative, who will forward it to you with a perfunctory cover letter and claim he has served his constituent. Such tactics are disinformation. The truth is not disclosed and the cover continues. The government still presumes your liability. If we fall prey to deceit, we are victims of obfuscation. Yet, with knowledge, we understand a proper context of tax law that is not what we originally believed.

When I was under civil and criminal investigation, I wrote to twelve government officials. Not one of them identified *the law* which made me liable to file a federal income tax return. I held a credible legal and lawful position that the tax code no longer applied to me.

In 2000, I rebutted in writing any government presumption. When my defense lawyers claimed my belief was "frivolous," that they could not argue it for fear of being sanctioned by the court, I expected the court to accept my own jurisdictional challenge and rebuttal of the government's presumption. Yet, the court denied my efforts and documents which validated my status under fundamental, the Constitution. The jury did not learn why *U.S. persons* are legally liable to the federal income tax and why I was no longer subject to limited congressional taxing authority.

Admittedly, having endured a nine-year criminal investigation and a federal tax trial, I would have prepared differently. If informed Americans effectively asserted their rebuttals of presumption, officials would avoid any revelation of the truth in a public forum. They would refuse to prosecute. This is the key; but it is also the greatest challenge. The federal government does not want to relinquish its rigid position or give credence that it has no authority over those who are without its jurisdiction. Moreover, defense attorneys do not want to argue a valid jurisdictional challenge.

Is there collusion between the government, defense attorneys, and courts that preclude evidence and beliefs which would inevitably reveal the true nature of the federal income tax? Officials have an incentive to prosecute and instill a fear that will guarantee compliance with the tax code. Officials must attack any challenge with a disinformation campaign that is sanctioned by the courts. Federal judges *will* avoid the revelation that Americans are not obligated to the income tax as defense attorneys willfully cower in fear and hide behind their "Code of Ethics." Yes, while we blindly accept that we have a sound legal process, Americans are denied justice. Convictions in tax cases are assured.

Americans must realize that all credible arguments which refute any liability for the federal income tax have been denied by the IRS. With a slew of deceptively written responses that are propped up by the three branches of the government as valid, the

IRS remains silent and unchallenged. Each branch wrongly presumes all IRS answers are correct. Each branch serves as a bulwark against both truth and justice.

This approach works nicely for the government. Any valid claim by an educated defendant will not reach the district courts. This keeps the argument from the appellate courts. If an argument cannot gain traction during appeal, the Supreme Court will neither defeat the IRS or government deception nor confirm the proper interpretation and limits of congressional taxing statutes. One need only refer to <u>Cheek v United States</u>, 498 US 192, (1991). The Supreme Court stated:

> ... the statutory term "willfully" as used in the federal criminal statutes... carv[ed] out an exception to the rule. [presumption that one knows the law.] This special treatment of criminal tax offenses is largely due to the complexity of the tax law. [brackets added]

The Court then stated,

> The proliferation of statutes and regulations has sometimes made it difficult for the average citizen to know and comprehend the extent of the duties and obligations imposed by the tax laws. Congress has accordingly softened the impact of the common-law presumption by making specific intent to violate the law an element of certain federal tax offenses.

The Court established that

> The **standard for** the statutory willfulness requirement is the **voluntary, intentional violation of a known legal duty**. Id. 201 **Willfulness**, as construed by our prior decisions in criminal tax cases, **requires the Government to prove that**

the law imposed a **duty to the defendant**, the defendant knew of this duty, and that he voluntarily and intentionally violated that duty. Id.

Given the <u>Cheek</u> case, the government must avoid a defendant stating a reasonable belief as to the proper representation of the tax laws into a court of record before a jury. Consider a District Court decision within the Fourth Circuit, four years after the <u>Cheek</u>, which quoted the Supreme Court.

> **We thus disagree** with the court of appeals' requirement **that a "claimed good faith belief must be objectively reasonable"** if it is to be considered as possibly **negating** the **Government's evidence** purporting to show a defendant's awareness of the legal duty at issue. 496 US at 203

The court stated,

> Thus, Cheek simply states that a **good faith belief of legality, no matter how unreasonable**, negates the statutory element of willfulness for tax evasion and failure to file a return, and that **a jury must be allowed to consider evidence of such a belief**. Id.

With this admonition, we may conclude that a reasonable belief *would* merit the scrutiny of any jury, as informed Americans defend themselves against the unreasonable claim of a federal income tax liability.

We must dignify the Supreme Court's portrayal that the tax statutes and regulations are "difficult for the average citizen to know and comprehend." For our purposes, we will define an "average citizen" as one with a sixth-grade education. When an American actually studies the tax law and understands the limits of congressional tax authority, we may appreciate why the

Department of Justice intends to deny jurors (*average citizens*) from learning anything contrary to their uninformed beliefs. This allows the government to soundly reject any reasonable argument as *frivolous*.

This leads to a defining thought. With the amount of research into tax law done by discerning Americans, there must be some veracity to their findings; otherwise, the government would not avoid their conclusions outright. Officials would not use the process, the supposed *justice* system, to prevent grounded beliefs from gaining a foothold in American and constitutional jurisprudence.

Since the government avoids any reasonable argument, we must reconcile such arguments have merit. While any given argument may not be fully vetted (the tax law is purposely complicated), should we avoid them? If we want to know the truth, if we want to understand the extent of the government's jurisdiction and subsequent deception, if we want to know the limits of congressional taxing power, we cannot do as we have always done, submit to government deceit out of fear.

If the federal government could not tax an American's earnings since the founding of this country in 1776 until the late 1930s, we must ask a reasonable query. What happened? Did Congress acquire vast reach over the American people and, if so, how? In The Rebutted Presumption, we discovered not just a theory, but that government codes, regulations, and manuals, along with court decisions, confirm the basis as to why a *United States person* is liable for the federal income tax and an American is not.

Armed with such information, we either remain in the comfort of our ignorance or we defeat government deception that instills fear. Moreover, we learned that jurisdiction, and not any presumed tax liability, is fundamental to limited power and our natural rights. If we don't challenge the jurisdiction upon which any official purports to act, we have lost the basis for our freedom. The Supreme Court stated,

> We have no more right to decline the exercise of jurisdiction which is given, than to usurp that which is not given. The one or the other would be treason to the Constitution. *Cohen v Virginia*, 6 Wheat 264, 404 (1821)

The people delegated power to the federal government to expressly distinguish its reach. Power which is used to the contrary is anathema to what is sacrosanct and essential to our rights and security.

If an educated American learned how and why he was not liable to and for the federal income tax, but he was unable to rely on any subsequent reasonable belief to defeat a criminal tax charge, would there be justice? A timeless maxim of justice states that without mens rea (evil intent) a man may not commit an actus reus (criminal act). The Supreme Court embraces this premise. If an informed American relies upon his reasonable belief that he is not liable for the federal income tax, would he have the mens rea needed to commit the crime of willful failure to file? No. If he did not have the evil intent, is there a crime? No.

If the *United States* does not have jurisdiction from the outset is the federal income tax the issue? If the income tax is not *the* priority, there must be an ulterior motive? Indisputably, the government must suppress the truth about jurisdiction to avoid any credible rebuttals to its presumption that it has authority. The government must perpetuate any and all deceit as it seeks pervasive compliance among all possible U.S. persons (Americans), which is achieved with criminal convictions of the innocent. In the end, deceit breeds confusion, which ensures ignorance, apathy, and, most importantly, fear.

Fear within the hearts and minds of the American people is assured within an unconstitutional process that is shielded, in part, by what is known as the "Administrative State."[24] Not only do the legislative, executive, and judicial branches avoid the constitutional construct of the American Republic, officials rely upon unilateral decisions and actions of its agencies, independent bodies which exercise power without accountability. This syndrome is described by Peter McCutchen in <u>MISTAKES, PRECEDENT, AND THE RISE OF THE ADMINISTRATIVE STATE TOWARD A CONSTITUTIONAL THEORY OF THE SECOND BEST</u>.[25]

A little over forty years ago, Justice Jackson characterized the rise of the administrative state as "probably the most significant legal trend of the last century."[1] He coined the term "Fourth Branch" to describe administrative agencies and contended that this fourth branch "has deranged our three-branch legal theories much as the concept of a fourth dimension unsettles our three-dimensional thinking."[2] Today, forty years later, our legal theories remain deranged. Current approaches to separation of powers problems remain inadequate to the task of coping with the administrative state.

The reason is simple. The structural Constitution[3] sets forth a system of government that allocates power among three departments.[4] This division is intended to ameliorate the corrupting effect of power. Thus, the powers delegated to each department are carefully limited in scope, and each of the three departments acts as a check on the power of the others. In Madison's justly famous words, "[a]mbition must be made to counteract ambition."[5] There is no room for a fourth branch within this tripartite scheme of governance. In exercising executive, legislative, and judicial power, administrative agencies combine powers that the Constitution separates; moreover, agencies are subject to none of the checks imposed upon the three traditional

---

[24] http://www.heritage.org/research/reports/2007/11/the-birth-of-the-administrative-state-where-it-came-from-and-what-it-means-for-limited
[25] http://scholarship.law.cornell.edu/cgi/viewcontent.cgi?article=2539&context

departments. In short, the administrative state is unconstitutional.

Nevertheless, the Supreme Court has not invalidated the post-New Deal administrative state as inconsistent with the constitutional text. The Court's unwillingness to do so is, in large part, pragmatic. Even if the Court were disposed to order the task of dismantling the federal bureaucracy, it might not have the political capital necessary to realize its objective. Moreover, to declare the administrative state unconstitutional would require the Court to overrule an immense and deeply rooted body of precedent. It is easy to understand that the Court would be unwilling to adopt a constitutional theory with such far-reaching implications.

*Bigelow Teaching Fellow and Lecturer in Law, University of Chicago Law School. J.D. 1990, Northwestern University School of Law. I would like to thank Terri Abruzzo, Bob Bennett, Michelle Browdy, John Donohue, Deirdre Fox, Melinda Hardy, Kathy Moriarty, and Cass Sunstein for their helpful thoughts and comments with respect to prior drafts of this Article. I am also extremely grateful to Gary Lawson, Tammy McCutchen, and Paula Stannard, each of whom took the time to do a detailed markup of a prior draft. Their comments-both substantive and editorial-went above and beyond the call of duty. Finally, I would like to thank Becky Adams and Kathi Ortiz for their excellent secretarial work.

1 Federal Trade Comm'n v. Ruberoid Co., 343 U.S. 470, 487 (1952) (Jackson, J., dissenting).

2 Id.

3 Traditionally, commentators have distinguished between structural provisions of the Constitution-which allocate powers among the various branches of government and between the federal and state governments-and individual

rights provisions-which guarantee individual rights. Some have argued that different interpretive methodologies are appropriate for analyzing these two different types of provisions. See MICHAEL, THE CONSTITUTION, THE COURT, AND HUMAN RIGHTS 37-60 (1982) (defending "noninterpretive" review of "human rights" provisions of the Constitution while rejecting such review with respect to separation of powers issues). Akhil Amar has criticized the distinction between structural and individual rights provisions, arguing that the Bill of Rights has significant structural components. See Akhil R. Amar, The Bill of Rights As a Constitution, 100 YALE L.J. 1131 (1991) (contending that the Bill of Rights and the structural constitution have more in common than is often believed). 4 I use the term "department" rather than the more commonly used term, "branch," because the Constitution does so. See Steven G. Calabresi & Kevin H. Rhodes, *The Structural Constitution: Unitary Executive, Plural Judiciary,* 105 HARV. L. REV. 1155, 1156 n.6 ("The Constitution uses the word 'Department' to refer to the three institutions of our national government."). 5 THE FEDERALIST No. 51 at 322 (James Madison) (Clinton Rossiter ed., 1961).

All three branches of government abjectly ignore what is unconstitutional in order to achieve a specific goal—control. We are a controlled people. Our wholesale refusal to accept this fact does not make it any less true. You may even rest upon the fact that I am a convicted felon as justification to disbelieve the content in this book. If this is the case, consider the work[26] written by a paralegal who not only confirms the material offered

---

[26] https://supremelaw.org/fedzone11/index.htm

in <u>The Rebutted Presumption</u>, he explains various facets in greater detail. Are you willing to discount his explanation?

The information in <u>The Rebutted Presumption</u> may pose a problem for the *average American*—one with a sixth-grade education. It may awaken those who have been willfully ignorant of the law. Freedom requires vigilance and vigilance is not an attribute of the ignorant and fearful.

How will this insight change your life? Will it alter how you view the tax system and, ultimately, your freedom? Will it affect what you do? As you live into a life of greater freedom, you may want more information. I encourage you to place a priority upon the issue of jurisdiction and then learn tax law. Jurisdiction is the key.

If you want the legal briefs I filed in court, especially during the post conviction process, and if you want an example of a rebuttal to the government's presumption, send an email to the publisher of this book. Please share this book with others. Begin a grand conversation. Probe into what was previously unknown. Expose the disinformation and reveal the truth. No matter how the math is done, 10,000 wrongs do not make a right and one man who asserts a right may not be wrong.

James B. Johnson
January 18, 2017

About the Author

James Bowers Johnson is the father of Cory, Heather, Timothy, and Emma. Born and raised in Virginia, he was graduated from the Virginia Military Institute in 1987. As a Distinguished Military Graduate, he received an Army Commission, served in the field of Military Intelligence and was Company Commander for HHC, 748th MI Battalion, 704th MI Brigade, INSCOM.

He was unjustly incarcerated for four years for allegedly failing to sign a piece of paper for the Federal Government. You may read about his incredible story in The End of Justice, a revelation as to why America is the most incarcerated country in the world. He also wrote The Ledge an insightful explanation as to how and why struggle and suffering are essential to life.